Sustainable Settlement in the Brazilian Amazon

Anna Luíza Ozório de Almeida*
and
João S. Campari**

Oxford University Press

OXFORD NEW YORK TORONTO
DELHI BOMBAY CALCUTTA MADRAS KARACHI
KUALA LUMPUR SINGAPORE HONG KONG TOKYO
NAIROBI DAR ES SALAAM CAPE TOWN
MELBOURNE AUCKLAND

and associated companies in

BERLIN IBADAN

Published by Oxford University Press, Inc.
200 Madison Avenue, New York, N.Y. 10016

Manufactured in the United States of America
First printing December 1995

The late Anna Luíza Ozório de Almeida was a staff member in the World Bank's
Education and Social Policy Department at the time of the writing of this
volume. Her co-author, João Campari, is a Ph.D. candidate in the Economics
Department of the University of Texas at Austin.

The findings, interpretations, and conclusions expressed in this study are entirely
those of the authors and should not be attributed in any manner to the World
Bank, to its affiliated organizations, or to members of its Board of Executive
Directors or the countries they represent.

Library of Congress Cataloging-in-Publication Data
Almeida, Anna Luíza Ozório de.
    Sustainable settlement in the Brazilian Amazon / Anna Luíza Ozório
de Almeida and João S. Campari.
        p. cm.
    Includes bibliographical references.
    ISBN 0-19-521104-9
        1. Land settlement—Amazon River Region. 2. Land settlement—
Brazil. 3. Sustainable agriculture—Amazon River Region.
4. Sustainable agriculture—Brazil. 5. Deforestation—Amazon River
Region. 6. Deforestation—Brazil. I. Campari, João S.
II. International Bank for Reconstruction and Development.
III. Title.
HD499.A44A457   1995
333.3'1811—dc20   .95-10600
                                                        CIP

Contents

Acknowledgments

This work began as a report for the position of Visiting Research Fellow in the Latin America and the Caribbean Environment Division of the World Bank from April to August 1992. Its objective is to discuss policy implications for the World Bank derived from empirical analysis of a panel of small farmers surveyed in 1981 and 1991 in directed colonization projects in the Brazilian Amazon.

Nancy Birdsall extended the original invitation for this research to be done at the World Bank. Dennis Mahar and Oey Astra Meesook provided encouragement and institutional support for the project. Other members of the Bank staff who were especially generous with their time and criticism were Sérgio Margulis, Carlos Primo Braga, and Robert Schneider. Hans Binswanger made many helpful comments, as did Michele de Nevers, John Dixon, Philip Hazelton, and William Partridge. Members of the Agriculture and Natural Resources, Agricultural Policies Division also gave helpful suggestions, especially Harold Alderman, Jock Anderson, Antônio Salazar Brandão, and Gershon Feder. Daniel Gross, Robert Kaplan, John Redwood, Alfredo Sfeir-Younis, and Shekhar Shah also helped us deal with different aspects of this research.

Meetings at the World Bank of the Brazil Agricultural and Resource Policy workshop, led by Malcolm Bale and Kreszentia Duer, provided stimulating discussions on many of the topics addressed in this text.

In addition, many presentations were made outside the World Bank at the invitation of Michael Conroy and Dan Slesnick (Department of Economics, the University of Texas at Austin); Betsy Kuznesof (University of Kansas); Richard Reed (Department of Anthropology, Trinity University, San Antonio, Texas); Rúbens Ricúpero (Brazilian Embassy); Gert Rosenthal (Economic Commission for Latin America and the Caribbean); Margaret Sarles (U.S. Foreign Service Institute); and Charles Wood (Population Center and Department of Sociology, the University of Texas at Austin), all of whom provided stimulating discussions and highlighted important aspects of this research.

Informal discussions with David Feeny (Centre for Health Economics and Policy Analysis at McMaster University); Richard Graham (the University of Texas at Austin); Donald Harris (Stanford University); Juan Carlos Lerda (Economic Commission for Latin America and the Caribbean); Henrique Monteiro de Barros (Organization of American States); Fredricka Santos and John Wilson (World Bank); C. Peter Timmer (Harvard Institute for International Development); Steve Vosti (International Food Policy Research Institute); and Peter J. Wilcoxen (Department of Economics, the University of Texas at Austin) helped sharpen different parts of the argument. Students in the course "The Economics of the Amazon" at the University of Texas at Austin provided many insightful criticisms and suggestions. We are also grateful to the reviewers for their insightful comments.

Several research assistants prepared the core factual basis for this research. At the World Bank, Pamela Stedman researched and organized an extensive annotated bibliography, while Alex Panagides did the painstaking work of splicing together the 1981 and 1991 samples, figuring out and running countless tests and estimations, and putting together the statistical appendices to this report. At the Institute of Applied Economic Research (IPEA) of the Brazilian Planning Ministry, Adriana Alves, Gustavo Gontijo, Manuel Augusto Magina, Paulo Arthur Moneto, Paulo Sérgio Monteiro, Carlos Ozorio de Almeida, Flávio Paim Freaza, Maria da Piedade Morais, and Luciano Sobrinho Porto, plus a large team of field researchers, organized the survey research and questionnaires and performed the basic programming on the data base for 1991. Ângela Moulin Penalva Santos, although conducting research of her own, took over the management of data retrieval for this project at IPEA. She also graciously provided special tabulations on frontier merchants for this work. Sergei Soares provided valuable unpublished information on fiscal revenues and transfers from federal to state and municipal governments in Brazil during the 1980s. Carlos Eduardo F. Young made detailed comments and suggestions on an earlier version, incorporated into this one. Roberto das Chagas Campos, Diva Rodrigues de Mattos, and Carlaile Pina Meireles at IPEA aided in typing, logistics, and communications. At the World Bank, Maria Abundo, Laura Alvarez, Christos Georgiou, and Bobak Rezaian walked us safely through the perilous jungle of office technology.

We are also grateful to the small farmers who endured our relentless questioning, as well as to all the kind people who helped us in the Amazon itself. We alone are responsible for any errors and omissions in the text and would welcome readers' comments and criticisms.

Foreword

This book is about small farmers in the Brazilian Amazon and how to raise their incomes while reducing resource degradation. The starting point of the book is the observation that whereas those farmers who deforested the Amazon during the 1970s and 1980s had migrated there from *outside* the basin, most of the small farmer deforesters of today have apparently come from *within* the region. Hence the greatest threat from small farmers to the Amazon forest is coming from intraregional migration. The central paradox is this: unsuccessful farmers tend to be unstable, selling out and moving on to new frontiers where they will deforest again. Parallel to this, successful farmers are led to increase deforestation in the place where they remain. The issue is thus no longer how to prevent migration to the Amazon from the rest of the country but how to ensure that farmers already in the Amazon stay where they have already deforested, thus reducing migration and deforestation farther inland. The main argument in the book is that intra-regional migration can be stemmed only by establishing sustainable farming in already deforested areas. Such sustainability would not likely attract interregional migrants because of irreversible changes that occurred during the 1980s in Brazil's population and economy.

A deliberate policy of Amazonian settlement was initiated in Brazil during the early 1970s in response to massive dislocations of poor farmers because of drought in the northeast and expulsion of tenants, squatters, and small landowners in the south. Over the next two decades, vast areas were deforested. In the 1990s a large part of the original settlers of the 1970s have left their plots, which are now increasingly owned by the local urban middle class. Some of those who left profited from the sale of their lands, but many were soon as poor as when they started. Thus, although much of Amazon deforestation has been done by small farmers, they have not necessarily kept the land they cleared.

Small farmers are encroaching upon Indian and forest reserves set up by federal and local governments—some with support from the World Bank, other international organizations, and nongovernmental organizations—and have even reached the political boundaries of Brazil, spilling over into neighboring countries. One approach for those concerned with environmental conservation would be to support obstructions to the migratory flow. Such conservationists may oppose infrastructure that is necessary for sustainable farming systems, such as roads and energy, social overhead investments, and any form of directed settlement. They may also encourage the establishment of forest reserves and increasingly protect them from encroachment. This approach has limitations, however. It does not address what is causing small farmers to leave old frontiers, and it bars them from the new ones they desperately need.

Increasing the sustainability of settlement in old Amazonian frontiers requires learning from the errors of the past, which led to unsustainable settlements, and avoiding those of the present, which oppose any new settlement. Based on original field panel data spanning two decades and representing the largest and most comprehensive data set ever produced on the economic variables that influence small farmer deforestation in the Amazon, this book makes a major contribution to the debate by outlining a policy prescription to increase the sustainability of small farming in the already settled parts of the Amazon. This approach amounts to a frontier poverty reduction program that uses economic policies to raise agricultural incomes and reduce environmental aggression. It requires environmental agencies to share in the design and enforcement of economic policy instruments and economic agencies to support environmental objectives. None of this can be achieved without the cooperation, and willingness to change, of all involved agencies, local and central, national and international, and governmental and nongovernmental, including the World Bank. Given the acceleration of intra-Amazonian migrations, institutional change is increasingly urgent.

This book was the last major piece of work that Anna Luíza Ozório de Almeida completed before she died in September 1994. As important as this book is, I want its readers to know how much of herself Anna Luíza gave to this book and how much it meant to her when she heard in June 1994 that it had been accepted for publication. I still have the electronic mail that she sent me from the hospital on August 9, 1994, saying how happy she was that the final manuscript had been approved and asking me to write the foreword for the book.

Anna Luíza was a very special person, and we were fortunate to have known her and to have worked with her. And she also collaborated on this book with someone special—João Campari—who has had to carry the final burden of seeing the manuscript to press.

Oey Astra Meesook
Manager, Poverty Analysis and Social Assistance
Povery and Social Policy Department
The World Bank
July 1995

Acronyms and Abbreviations

bóias-frias	poor urban dwellers who earn their living working in the fields
benfeitorias	physical improvements made on farms
cabloclo	type of indigenous technology
CELADE	Centro Latinoamericano de Demografia
CPD	Centro de Processamento de Dados
DPE	Diretoria de Pesquisas (de IBGE)
FAO	Food and Agricultural Organisation of the UN
FPM	Fundo de Participação dos Municípios
GEF	Global Environment Facility
GTA	Grupo de Trabalho da Amazônia
IBAMA	Instituto Brasileiro do Meio Ambiente e Recursos Naturais Renováveis
IBGE	Fundacão Instituto Brasileiro de Geografia e Estatística
imediatismo	high rates of time preference of small farmers
INCRA	Instituto Nacional de Colonização e Reforma Agrária
INPA	Instituto Nacional de Pesquisas Amazônicas
IPEA	Instituto de Pesquisa Econômica Aplicada
MARA	Ministério da Agricultura e Reforma Agrária
MIRAD	Ministério da Reforma Agrária e Desenvolvimento
minifundiários	small landholders
NGOs	nongovernmental organizations

PNUD/BRA	Programa das Nações Unidas para o Desenvolvimento/Brasil
Polonoroeste	Programa de Desenvolvimento Integrado do Noroeste do Brasil (integrated development program for northwest region of Brazil)
PROBOR	Programa de Incentivo à Produção de Borracha
SAFEM	Sistema de Acompanhamento das Finanças dos Estados e Municípios
SIVAM	Serviço de Informação e Vigilância da Amazônia
UFRJ/USP	Universidade Federal do Rio de Janeiro/Universidade de São Paulo
UNDP	United Nations Development Programme

CHAPTER 1

Introduction and Principal Findings

The current migration of small farmers from old to new frontiers within the Amazon poses an important threat to the forest. In the long run, such intraregional migration—which is increasing and spilling out over Brazil's borders—will eventually put pressure on forest reserves now being established in the Amazon by local and federal governmental agencies. Some of these reserves are being organized with substantial international resources and World Bank support. In order to protect forest reserves from future encroachment, agriculturally sustainable frontiers must be promoted in conjunction with direct forest conservation projects.

Speculative demand for land by a growing, prosperous Amazonian middle class is one of the important forces impelling growing numbers of small farmers to sell their plots and move on to settle temporarily and deforest new frontiers. In response to the national economic crisis during the 1980s, an emergent, local, urban middle class increasingly began buying frontier land—originally deforested by the pioneers of the 1970s—for the purpose of holding it as a store of value. The potential gains from speculation in the frontier land markets came to compete, therefore, with the land's agricultural potential, and few small farmers withstood the pressure to sell. Those who did not were mainly the outstandingly productive, whose profits were plowed back into expanding agriculture, and the outstandingly indebted, whose repayment obligations locked them into their shrinking farms.

Small farmers in the Amazon have been responding to economic conditions that reward speculation and encourage deforestation. Without new policies designed to change these conditions, therefore, the 1990s will probably witness continued deforestation, fueled by growing intraregional expulsions and migrations. The basic policy prescription that emerges from this work is that Amazonian deforestation can be reduced by inverting current economic rewards for speculation and intraregional migration so that farmers are discouraged from selling their cleared land and moving on to clear forest farther inland and from deforesting more extensively their current plots. In this book, a prescription that promotes agriculturally sustainable frontiers is combined with the judicious use of pricing and fiscal policies in order to elevate agricultural productivity, punish speculation in land transactions, and penalize deforestation directly in the Brazilian Amazon. Ideally, such policies must be created and enforced at the local level and be flexible enough to deal with a variety of Amazonian circumstances. (The cost of decentralization would be efficiency variations across locations.) The policies should also generate sufficient local revenues to pay for their enforcement, as well as for the expenses of direct conservation measures, such as demarcation and protection of native Indian, extractive, biological, and other reserves. New local taxes on capital gains, agricultural income (from farms above a certain size), fallow land, and stumpage could be established toward this end. The federal government could serve in a coordinating capacity, and the World Bank, other international organizations, and nongovernmental organizations (NGOs) could provide technical and financial assistance.

Based on original recent field data, this work outlines a policy prescription to increase the sustainability of small farming in the already settled parts of the Amazon. This approach amounts to a frontier poverty reduction program that uses economic policies to raise agricultural incomes and reduce environmental aggression. It requires environmental agencies to share in the design and enforcement of economic policy instruments and economic agencies to support environmental objectives. None of this can be achieved without the cooperation, and willingness to change, of all involved agencies, local and central, national and international, and governmental and nongovernmental, including the World Bank. Given the acceleration of the intra-Amazonian migrations, institutional change is increasingly urgent.

Success in this area will require that local and federal governments, as well as international organizations, work with local people in order to develop institutions that will support the innovative use of policy to achieve environmental ends. It is of equal importance that good farming settlements not attract a new wave of interregional migrants in a perverse demonstration effect. This does not appear likely. The economic and demographic adjustments that originally led to declining interregional migration in the 1980s have probably become irreversible, indicating that eventual recovery from Brazil's current economic crisis will probably not trigger another Amazon-bound migration comparable to that of the 1970s.

This work also discusses two other important issues: the relationship between Amazonian deforestation and general macroeconomic conditions in Brazil, and the relationship between returns to frontier farming and the cost to the global economy of reducing Amazonian deforestation. Although the original intention of this work was not to address either question, empirical findings bear upon these issues in important ways.

Macroeconomic instability appears to fuel deforestation in two ways. On the one hand, it drives up land prices and/or changes the demand for land from that of a productive factor into that of a speculative asset. This shift leads to the buying and hoarding of land by the nonfarming middle class, and the small farmers are pushed farther into the forest. On the other hand, low wages and the low probability of finding a job in a depressed urban economy reduce the opportunity cost of frontier farming, encouraging settlers to continue farming and deforesting the frontier. On both counts, therefore, economic recovery may tend to reduce deforestation in the Amazon.

The cost to the global economy of reducing deforestation may turn out to be much higher than land prices alone would suggest. Farmers manage a portfolio of agricultural, nonagricultural, and speculative incomes, not all of which get capitalized into frontier land prices. Since in many frontier locations agricultural income is a small and declining part of total household income, the income forgone when land is sold is greater than the net present value of the income derived from agricultural production alone. Additionally, frontier farmers' transactions in varied markets sustain a large and growing nonfarming economy, inside and outside the Amazon. This contingent would also forgo income if Amazonian land were to be kept out of agricultural production. So the cost to the global economy of containing Amazonian deforestation is underestimated if the full range of forgone incomes is not taken into account.

These conclusions are based upon an analysis of twenty years of Amazonian settlement in Brazil, using secondary data, institutional interviews, surveys of the literature, and a large panel survey of small farmers (500), merchants (100), and institutions (80) in representative settlement projects in the Brazilian Amazon. Farmers, merchants, and institutions were interviewed in 1981 and 1991 in public projects in the state of Pará and private projects in the state of Mato Grosso. This sample captured much of the large differences across settlement locations and highlighted some broad underlying processes. Differences appeared in natural resources; in political, legal, and institutional frameworks; and in settler origin characteristics, including economic and cultural ties.

Background of Amazonian Settlement

Since colonial times, Brazil has dealt with the social problem of landlessness by extending the agricultural frontier westward. Successive federal and state-level land distribution agencies, such as the National Institute for Colonization and Agrarian Reform (INCRA) and the former Ministry of Agriculture and Agrarian Reform (MIRAD), have traditionally been responsible for bringing together agrarian reform and colonization. Rather than tackle the political cost of taking from wealthy landowners and giving to the landless poor, land distribution in Brazil has mostly taken from nature and given to the rich. Directed colonization projects are the exception to this rule.

For the last few years, since the rapid rise and fall of MIRAD in the mid-1980s, the issue of government-directed, small farmer settlements has lain relatively dormant in Brazil in general and in the Amazon in particular. Experience gained in the 1970s and 1980s, whether with colonization projects in the frontier or agrarian reform projects (*assentamentos de reforma agrária*) in established areas, was disappointing. Many directed settlements, though made in the name of distribution, quickly regressed into consolidated and concentrated land property structures whose social benefit was questioned by leading domestic and foreign policy communities. In addition, massive deforestation and inappropriate tropical farming technologies that caused soil degradation generated conservationists' outcry against the environmental impact of colonization projects.

Small farmer settlement, however, is likely to become a governmental priority again soon under the pressure that arises from rural violence and because of a growing local demand for stabilization. Since the end of the military regime in 1985, the rural workers' unions, once severely repressed, have become larger, more widespread, and better organized. Landowners' associations have become more influential as well. The low priority in the allocation of government resources to land distribution policies in recent years has escalated the conflict between these two groups. An increasing incidence of violence has followed not only in the Amazon but also throughout Brazil, as landless farmers press for, and landowners resist, any form of land redistribution.

Since the promulgation of the 1988 constitution, fiscal reform and increasing decentralization of the government have given more power to local Amazonian communities that benefit by settlement schemes. Demand for colonization is a growing political issue in local and regional elections. Small farm surveys in the Amazon and in the rest of Brazil are showing that the distributive effects of directed colonization projects are greater and more long-lasting than was once believed. The errors of the past have been learned, and top-down, unassisted, federal colonization projects that spread unsustainable farming over land areas too large to manage are recognized as being undesirable; the movement is toward local-level programs aimed at relieving poverty and social conflict.

Principal Findings

The aim of this project was to attain long-term and generalizable policy implications from an original longitudinal data set, while taking into account the variability of the Amazonian experience. Chapters 2 and 3 provide background on the evolution of population and economic conditions in

Brazil during the 1980s. Chapters 4 and 5 analyze a large panel survey conducted in 1981 and 1991 of small farmers in representative locations of the Amazon frontier. The originality of the work as a whole lies in the unique primary information it brings to light on the evolution of frontier farming in the Brazilian Amazon during the 1980s.

Chapter 2 uses Brazilian demographic and economic census to trace the path of migrations to and within the Amazon during the 1970s and 1980s. Small farmers who deforested the Amazon during the 1970s and 1980s had mostly migrated there from *outside* the basin. Most small farmer deforesters of the 1990s have apparently come from *within* the region, however. The greatest threat from small farmers to the Amazon forest, therefore, now seems to come from intraregional migrations. The issue is no longer how to prevent deforesting farmers from migrating to the Amazon from the rest of the country, but how to ensure that farmers already in the Amazon stay where they have already deforested, thus reducing migration (and deforestation) farther inland. Intraregional migration can be stemmed only by establishing sustainable farming in already deforested areas. Chapter 2 argues that the Amazon is not likely to suffer overwhelming population influx from outside the region. Fertility rates for Brazil are declining, overall and regional population growth rates are falling, a general process of urbanization is under way, and experience from the past two decades has taught migrants that settling the Amazon is arduous. On the other hand, rural exodus is accelerating within the Amazon itself.

Chapter 3 uses fiscal and other sources, plus direct field research among Amazonian merchants in 1991 to analyze the growth of the public and private sectors in the Amazon during the 1980s. The chapter shows that economic conditions shifted dramatically during the 1980s, inside and outside the Amazon, changing the course of intraregional migrations. As the national economic conditions weakened and the federal government weakened, local economies grew and provincial governments became stronger.

The transition to democracy and fiscal decentralization brought far more revenues into the Amazon via local governments than were lost with the demise of federal fiscal incentives, credit incentives, and other programs. Meanwhile, primary activities in the frontiers of the 1970s shifted from agroextractive to a form of urban ranching in the 1980s. By the 1990s, a large part of the original settlers of the 1970s had left their plots, which are now increasingly owned by the local urban middle class. Some of those who left profited from the sale of their lands, but many were soon as poor as they started. Thus, though much of Amazon deforestation has been done by small farmers, they have not necessarily kept the land they cleared. The new urban middle class, linked by trade to the industrial Southeast, started to purchase local land as a store of value mainly in response to the national economic crisis. These urbanites constitute a local elite that may offer resistance to the policy changes this work recommends.

econometrics, resource and environmental economics, institutional economics, public finance, economic demography, and others—to offer a policy prescription for reducing Amazon deforestation.

The empirical section of the book (chapters 4 and 5) assess how well, or how badly, small farmers are covering their opportunity costs of frontier farming. These opportunity costs are rather abstract. Overall, they represent alternative rates of remuneration of factors of production in the economy as a whole. Concrete alternatives, such as gold prospecting, drugs, extractivism, and so on, are not dealt with explicitly. Some terms are used interchangeably in the text, glossing over important differences, such as "frontier farmers," "settlers," "colonists," and "pioneers." The terms "Amazon," "Amazonia," and "the North region" are also substituted for one another, as are "family farming," "poor farming," and "small farming."

The most difficult notion to pin down was that of "sustainability," a term both overused and misused in the development literature. Instead of attempting to redefine the notion, the conceptual framework used in this book allows for a method that identifies movements toward and away from sustainability; that is, sustainability is said to increase as the ratio of private benefits to environmental costs rises and to decrease as the ratio declines. As used here, the term has a time dimension, as do policies aimed at changing farmer behavior to increase sustainability. The originality of this work lies in its empirical observation of indicators of changes in sustainability.

Empirical findings of the work bear upon some broader policy issues, such as how Amazonian deforestation relates to general macroeconomic conditions and the global economy. The evidence suggests the following:

- Recovery from economic depression in Brazil may be conducive to decreasing deforestation in the Amazon because (a) stabilization would reduce speculative demand for land and compress capital gains to small farmers in selling out and moving inland, and (b) if recovery creates jobs and raises wages, it would increase the opportunity cost of frontier farming, thus reducing the pressure of small farmers on the forest. The relationship between the environment and macroeconomic conditions is thus a complex one, subject to specific local conditions.
- The cost to the world economy of buying Amazonian land to prevent deforestation may be considerably greater than expected because (a) in selling land, frontier farmers forgo not only agricultural income, but also a whole portfolio of agricultural, nonagricultural, and speculative incomes and (b) farmers' transactions generate nonagricultural incomes inside and outside the Amazon that would also be forgone. The relationship between the environment and the global economy is thus also a complex one, subject to national and local conditions.

There are several things that this study does not attempt to do. It does not analyze data on Amazonian occupation as a whole, or on the general process of Amazon deforestation, beyond that caused by small farmers. It does not discuss some of the broader consequences of Amazonian deforestation, such as its global environmental impact or the political and social dimensions of Amazonian deforestation. (However, extensive reference to the literature is made.) Although the text does not attempt to offer an in-depth analysis of human capital, the data set used does contain information that pertains here. Ozório de Almeida (1992) offers more extensive research in this area. Likewise, health conditions, which are not explicitly examined in the text but are known to correlate to economic performance, are taken into account in the book's conclusions. Finally, it was not possible to undertake an empirical qualitative analysis of the soils of sampled locations. There is no evidence, however, that the colonization projects sampled have endogenized soil quality. The sample, therefore, is not biased in regard to soil type. To cover all of the above was beyond the scope of our study.

This book raises issues heretofore unexplored in the literature and is largely based on observations made in the Amazon in the 1970s and 1980s. The new information and novel interpretations it offers are based on an analysis of the largest and most complete data set ever produced on the economic variables that influence small farmers in the Amazon. Such observation of the economic behavior of a panel of small farmers over a span of twenty years, from the major thrust toward Amazonian colonization in the early 1970s until the chaotic aftermath of the early 1990s, is unprecedented (see appendix B for a description of procedures).

The main lesson learned is that changing Amazonian sustainability is an intra-Amazonian matter; interregional migrations no longer pose the threat they once did. If frontier farmers are not settled where they are now, they will eventually move to areas currently being placed under reserve. Conservation of these areas, therefore, will not be possible unless intraregional migrations are stopped. To increase sustainability, the Amazonian region must be viewed as whole over the long term.

The compartmentalization of academic knowledge, executive agencies, and financing institutions makes it very difficult to deal with the problem of Amazonian deforestation in its full complexity. Targeted lending operations and grants tend to focus on specific localities and to neglect overall processes that in the long run are necessary if individual projects are to succeed. This work addresses several issues that are generally overlooked. These are:

- the current intraregional nature of migrations to new frontiers,
- the importance of good farming in old frontiers for containing deforestation in new frontiers,
- the need for innovative economic-agronomic-environmental-social policies and institutional change at all levels, including at the World Bank, to ensure that Amazonian settlement becomes sustainable,

- the role of local governments, organizations, and communities in enforcing such policies.

By revealing the economic mechanisms at work in deforesting the Amazon today, we hope to contribute to the design of appropriate policies for use by the World Bank, other international organizations, and national and regional governments. Summoning the political will to implement such policies will depend on the recognition that they are necessary. This recognition is all that we are trying to accomplish. If we can do this, then further analysis, debate, negotiation, and experience should build the political will necessary to achieve effective implementation.

Note

1. The term "agricultural involution" is used throughout this book to indicate a decline in the quality of farming by frontier settlers. When farming covers its opportunity costs, settlers tend toward "evolution," meaning they improve as farmers and are likely to remain on the land. When the opportunity costs of farming rise, settlers tend toward "involution"; they stop being good farmers and may eventually sell out and leave the land.

It is important to note that we are not using "agricultural involution" as Clifford Geertz used it in his book by that title. That author used the term to refer to the development of labor-intensive rice cultivation in Asia. He applied that concept with precision to the phenomenon to which he was referring. It is important to note that in this book we are making use of the same term with equal precision to refer to a different phenomenon.

Another observation worth noting is that agricultural involution does not necessarily mean abandonment. Abandonment of the plot does not occur immediately when opportunity costs turn against frontier farming. A form of low-level equilibrium farming begins, which, if compared to that which prevailed previous to farmers' arrival, characterizes "involution." A frontier is a dynamic place, and comparisons in time must be made. Agricultural involution compares negatively to the farming that was there before. Abandonment may or may not occur in consequence.

CHAPTER 2

Population Shifts in the Amazon during the 1980s

It is widely believed that the pressure of a growing population in the Amazon is causing the destruction of the rain forest. Conservation would thus require reducing the size of such population or, at least, not attracting new entrants. This is not realistic, however. The Amazon population now numbers more than 19 million people, about one-third of whom live in rural areas and show no intention of leaving the region. Forced relocation in such massive numbers would be impossible since neither resources nor the political will to do so exist. Any realistic Amazon conservation scheme, therefore, must deal with the fact that for the foreseeable future, there will be approximately six million people farming the Amazon.[1] The issue, then, is how to do so sustainably.

The purpose of this chapter is to show that Amazon deforestation is largely responding to intraregional population shifts and to local-level dynamics, as opposed to countrywide pressures. Fertility rates for Brazil are declining, overall and regional rates of population growth are falling, and a general process of urbanization is under way. As a result, in the near future, Amazonian settlement is not expected to experience significant population pressure from the outside. Rural exodus, however, is accelerating within the Amazon, and small farming is becoming less sustainable. Both these factors have spurred intra-Amazonian migrations and deforestation farther inland to the very borders of Brazil, where farmers are adding to the flow of prospectors and other migrants now spilling over into neighboring countries. Thus, reduction of population pressure on the forest requires policies that curb intraregional rather than interregional migrations.

Fertility Decline

High fertility is often believed to contribute to pressure on fragile environments by creating a large stock of potential migrants. Rising fertility rates would suggest, other factors holding constant, a possible increase in the

Table 2.1 Population, Percentages, and Average Rates of Growth: Brazil and Regions (1960–91)

Area considered	Population					Percentage over country's total				Average annual geometric growth rate		
	1960	1970	1980	1991	Growth 1960–91	1960	1970	1980	1991	1960–70	1970–80	1980–91
Frontier												
North	2,561,782	3,603,860	6,619,317	10,146,218	7,584,436	3.65	3.87	5.57	6.94	3.47	5.02	3.96
Center-West	2,963,715	5,099,787	6,805,746	9,419,896	6,456,168	4.23	5.47	5.72	6.45	5.58	3.99	3.00
Total	5,525,497	8,703,647	13,425,063	19,566,114	14,040,617	7.88	9.34	11.29	13.39	4.65	4.43	3.48
Other regions												
Northeast	22,181,880	28,111,927	34,812,356	42,387,328	20,205,448	31.65	30.17	29.25	29.00	2.40	2.16	1.81
Southeast	30,630,728	39,853,498	51,734,125	62,121,357	31,490,629	43.70	42.78	43.47	42.50	2.67	2.64	1.68
South	11,753,075	16,496,493	19,031,162	22,079,703	10,326,628	16.77	17.71	15.99	15.11	3.45	1.44	1.36
Total	64,565,683	84,461,918	105,577,643	126,588,388	62,022,705	92.12	90.66	88.71	86.61	2.72	2.26	1.66
Brazil	70,091,180	93,165,565	119,002,706	146,154,502	76,063,322	100.0	100.0	100.0	100.0	2.89	2.48	1.89

Source: IBGE, *Censos Demográficos*, various years.

propensity to migrate, whereas declining fertility rates would suggest a decrease. These hypothesized relationships have not held in Brazil during the past thirty years, however.

The weighted averages of total fertility rates for Brazil were 5.6 for 1965, 3.2 for 1990, and the projected rate for 2000 is 2.4. The presumed year of achieving a reproduction rate of 1 is 2005. These figures indicate that the overall fertility rate has been falling and will probably continue to decline in the 1990s to less than half of what it was in the 1960s.[2] Despite important regional differentials (as described by Martine 1992b, page 17), this decline has been significant in all regions and social classes.[3] The drop in fertility rates, however, has *not* resulted in a reduction in the rates of migration and urban growth. On the contrary, during the 1960s and 1970s throughout much of the country, internal migration has remained high despite severe declines in fertility rates.

Internal migrations, in general, and to the Amazon in particular, seem to have been spurred more by economic and social factors than by population increase.[4]

The Populous Frontier

From 1960 to 1991 the growth of total population in the old *cerrado* frontier[5] and in the new Amazon frontier was more than 14 million people (see table 2.1).

During the 1980–91 period, however, rates of population growth significantly decreased in all regions relative to the previous decade. This phenomenon can be largely attributed to the general decline in fertility rates. Table 2.1 shows that, although the population growth rates for the North and the Center-West were relatively high in the 1980–91 period, these rates experienced the greatest declines relative to the 1970s. The *cerrado* frontier of the Center-West had the highest rates of population growth during its heyday in the 1960s, as did the Amazonian frontier during the 1970s. Since then, both regions have experienced far lower population growth rates.

These trends suggest that, until the early 1980s, migrations from old to new frontiers were *interregional*, from the *cerrado* and from other regions to the Amazon.[6] Nowadays, migrations from old to new frontiers seem to have become an *intraregional*, Amazonian phenomenon.

The Urban Frontier

Ever since the 1960s, the urban population in the frontier has grown at a much higher rate than the rural population (see Martine 1992b for detailed data). The frontier, therefore, is no exception to the process of urbanization that has been occurring throughout Brazil since the 1960s.[7] What is unique about Amazonian urbanization, however, is that it occurs despite a low population density of 0.23 inhabitants per square kilometer in the region as a whole.[8] For this reason, Amazonian urbanization may be considered precocious[9] (see table 2.2 and Ozório de Almeida 1991b, p. 622).

During the 1980s, frontier urbanization gained momentum. Shrinking opportunities in frontier agriculture stimulated the massive migration of would-be settlers to the region's cities and gave rise to an urban network more geographically balanced overall.[10]

Urbanization, therefore, is an overriding demographic tendency nation-wide, against which frontier expansion is but a weak countertrend. Increasingly, potential colonists choose to earn a living in urban settings, rather than venture into the forest. Nowadays, the significance of the shifting frontier tends to come less from its demographic, agricultural, and social magnitudes than from its environmental consequences.

Shifting Agricultural Frontier

The Brazilian agricultural frontier has historically been short-lived. (Ozório de Almeida 1992 and Sawyer 1990 expand on this point.) The main sending areas, once frontier areas themselves, soon began expelling emigrants at rates greater than those at which they were taking in immigrants. During the 1970s, the total growth of the rural population in the frontier was 1,281,575 as opposed to 1,325,223 in the previous decade (see table 2.2).[11]

During the 1960s and 1970s, the geographical spread of occupied frontier areas was considerable. As the frontier shifted, it left behind low-density population pockets where small farming activities had once been carried out. Small landowners sold their plots, either moving farther inland to reestablish their family farming or going to nearby towns, seeking nonfarm employment. Small tenants and squatters were evicted, and commercial agriculture took over, often converting farmland into pasture.[12]

Table 2.3 shows broad trends during successive decades. During the 1960–70 period, the Southeast experienced the greatest rural exodus in Brazil, the rural population declining by 1,224,574 persons. During the 1970–80 period, rural exodus in the Southeast increased but was topped by the exodus in the South, where the rural population declined by 2,023,200

Table 2.2 Variation in Rural Population in Frontier Areas, 1960–80

Frontier area	1960–70	1970–80
Amazon	547,745	1,047,912
Cerrado	777,478	233,668
Total	1,325,223	1,281,565

Source: IBGE, *Censos Demográficos* 1980, 1970, 1960, and Ozório de Almeida 1992.

Table 2.3 **Variation in Rural Population by Region, 1960–80**

Region	1960–70	1970–80
North	383,076	924,532
Northeast	1,945,981	957,853
Center-West	720,432	−178,430
Southeast	−1,224,574	−1,963,936
South	1,826,351	−2,023,200
All Brazil	3,651,266	2,283,181

Source: IBGE, *Censos Demograficos* 1980, 1970, 1960, and Ozório de Almeida 1992.

persons. This massive rural exodus in the South-Southeast during the 1960s and 1970s was caused by a number of factors, including the penetration of soybean and sugarcane plantations, changes in land laws and rural labor legislation, the effect of business cycle variations on real estate appreciation, and fiscal and credit policies favoring large farmers.[13]

The tables and map 2.1 show that during the 1970s the Center-West became an old frontier, expelling more farmers from the countryside than it absorbed, especially in the states of Mato Grosso do Sul and Goias.[14] Map 2.1 is based on the agricultural census and refers to units of agricultural production. Given that bean cultivation is strongly associated with small farmers, a reduction in the area harvesting this crop, as indicated by the dark area in the map, implies a decline of small farming. This is what occurred in the *cerrado* frontier during the 1970s. Unfortunately, the lack of 1991 census information on rural population makes comparison impossible for the 1980s (see Ozório de Almeida 1992, chapter 2, for further data).

Hollow Frontier

This section attempts to trace the movements of small farmers in the Amazon during the 1980s by looking at similarities between their movement and the area harvested with beans during the 1970s. Map 2.2 suggests rural population trends for the 1980s.

According to this map, the size of the intra-Amazonian rural exodus assumed impressive proportions during the 1980s.[15] The centripetal force of this exodus created a demographic hollow at the core of the frontier as it pushed migrants away from the Trans-Amazonian highway, which had drawn them in one decade before. Migrants concentrated in northern Mato Grosso and along national boundaries, often going beyond them into eight neighboring countries.[16] Elsewhere in the country, as noted by Martine (1992a and b), there was an inverse tendency to this intraregional post-frontier phenomenon: rural areas increased their absorption of small farm-

Map 2.1

IBRD 27149

BRAZIL
HARVESTED AREAS—BEANS—1970-75

PERCENT VARIATION:

- >500
- 100–500
- 50–99
- 0–49
- <0
- NON-PROJECT AREAS
- ⊛ NATIONAL CAPITAL
- ----- STATE BOUNDARIES
- —-·— INTERNATIONAL BOUNDARIES

0   500   1000 KILOMETERS
0   200   400   600 MILES

The boundaries, colors, denominations and any other information shown on this map do not imply, on the part of The World Bank Group, any judgment on the legal status of any territory, or any endorsement or acceptance of such boundaries.

NOVEMBER1995

Note: The dark areas in the northwestern part of the Brazilian Amazon indicate a long-term decline in extractive activity, mainly rubber tapping, and urbanization in the region. This is a pre-frontier phenomenon; it is very different from the post-frontier phenomenon in which farmer migration rapidly emptied the frontiers.

Source: Ozório de Almeida (1992).

Map 2.2

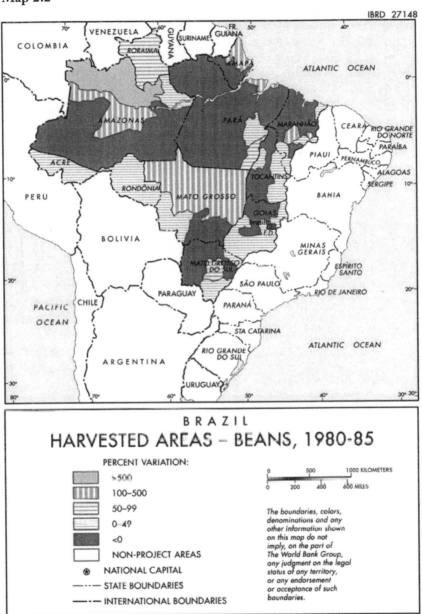

IBRD 27148

BRAZIL

HARVESTED AREAS - BEANS, 1980-85

PERCENT VARIATION:

- >500
- 100–500
- 50–99
- 0–49
- <0
- NON-PROJECT AREAS
- ⊛ NATIONAL CAPITAL
- ----- STATE BOUNDARIES
- —-— INTERNATIONAL BOUNDARIES

The boundaries, colors, denominations and any other information shown on this map do not imply, on the part of The World Bank Group, any judgment on the legal status of any territory, or any endorsement or acceptance of such boundaries.

NOVEMBER 1995

Source: Ozório de Almeida (1992).

ers. Map 2.2 shows that, during the early 1980s, even the *cerrado* frontier of the Center-West reabsorbed the bean-producing (small) farmers who had left this area during the 1970s. In the absence of a 1991 agricultural census, why small farming has been making a comeback is not yet understood. The issue is an important one, however, not only in its own right, but also for interpreting the intra-Amazonian rural exodus of the 1980s.

This exodus probably has intra-Amazonian causes, including the chronic itinerancy of frontier farmers and the unsustainability of frontier settlement. Although it is difficult to change such a long-lived, century-old phenomenon, the urgency of doing so is increasing, as the ecological and geographical limits of the frontier are being exhausted.[17] Sustainable settlement of small farmers in the Amazon is now imperative, not only to preserve the unexploited portion of the forest, but also to maintain good international relations with Brazil's neighbors.

Summary and Policy Implications

Based on the most recent data set available, the present chapter showed that (1) national and regional fertility rates are declining; (2) overall and regional rates of population growth are falling; (3) a process of precocious urbanization of the frontier has been under way for a long time and may be accelerating; (4) old frontiers in the *cerrado* and in the eastern and southern parts of the country have begun to reabsorb small farmers; and (5) the shifting Amazonian agricultural frontier is adding to pressures from prospectors and other migrant groups and emptying out vast areas that once attracted settlements. Given the large population in the Amazon and the rapidity with which this frontier population shifts, there is an urgent need for policies that could contribute to increasing the sustainability of Amazonian settlement.

Notes

1. Several recent authors (Partridge and Schumann 1989) assert that peasant farmers are not the main agents of forest clearance. Both Denevan (1978, page 67) and Foweraker (1981, page 208), on the other hand, argue that peasants do clear most of the original forest, which then passes on to cattle ranchers. In fact, small farmers occupy a smaller area than any other deforester in the Amazon. In 1980, for instance, total cropped area covered only 1 percent of total Amazon area, as compared to 4 percent covered by ranching (Ozório de Almeida 1992). However, in spite of this apparent insignificance, small farmers are the most mobile of deforesters; so over their lifetimes they clear an area far larger than what they currently occupy.

A simple numerical example illustrates this point. According to *World Resources* (1992, table 19.1), during the 1981–85 period, the yearly rate of deforestation in the Amazon was approximately 0.5 percent of total area in the basin. Dividing total cropped area (1 percent) by total yearly deforested area (0.5 percent) implies that crops remain, on average, only two years on each deforested plot. Many farmers, even small farmers, use their lands for considerably longer periods of time, as will be seen in chapter 4. So the underutilization of, and turnover on, deforested plots in the Amazon is very high indeed. In this sense, the most effective way to reduce small farmer deforestation would be to increase the duration of farming on each deforested plot. This is the thesis of this book and, in particular, the focus of chapter 4.

2. Quoting from a 1992 internal World Bank report: "Until the mid-1970s, Brazil had a pro-natalist policy. After that, its laissez-faire stance opened the way to considerable activity by NGOs...which were active in public education to popularize and legitimize family planning.... The contraceptive pill was mainly provided by private pharmacies whose prices were very low.... The social security health system paid for Caesarean deliveries, which provided an opportunity for tubal ligation as a side arrangement, for an additional payment." From the mid-1970s on, therefore, concerted efforts were made to reduce the fertility rate in Brazil.

3. For a discussion of urban growth in Brazil, see Martine (1992b). IBGE has data concerning regional decline in fertility rates.

4. In support of this position, see Martine (1992b, especially page 9) and Sawyer (1990, page 14). Contrary to this position, see Thiele (1990, introduction).

5. The *cerrado* region is basically a savanna ecosystem that covers most of the Center-West. The Amazon frontier consists mostly of tropical rainforest soils.

6. See Ozório de Almeida (1992, chapters 2 and 12) for a discussion of the literature and evidence on interregional migration and the advancing agricultural frontier. For a discussion of how migration during the 1970s affected deforestation—especially that caused by small farmers—see Browder (1988).

7. A thorough historical review of the urbanization process in Brazil can be found in Martine and Camargo (1983) and Martine (1992a and b). These sources analyze the impact of urban growth at the regional level, focusing particularly on frontier areas.

8. See table 2.1 and Ozório de Almeida (1991b, page 622).

9. In general, rapid urbanization occurs in the face of high population density. By precocious, we mean the process of urbanization that occurs despite low regional population density.

10. For a discussion of the impact of urban growth on local populations, refer to Moran (1983) and Penalva Santos (1993).

11. Unfortunately, because data on rural population are still not available from the population census of 1991, the 1980s are not included in table 2.2 This section does refer, however, to the 1985 agricultural census.

12. For a microeconomic model that discusses the conversion of land, given tenure insecurity, see Southgate and Pearce (1988). For a detailed analysis of the evolution of agriculture in the North during the 1970s, see Brito and Une (1987).

13. See Ozório de Almeida (1992, chapter 12) for a review of this literature, and Mesquita and Silva (1987b and c) for an account of the emergence of soybean plantations in the South and its impact on small farmers.

14. For a discussion of recent population movement on the frontier, see Ozório de Almeida (1992), Sawyer (1990), and Martine (1992a).

15. The methodology and data for constructing this map are the same as for map 2.1, but with data from the 1980 and 1985 agricultural censuses.

16. See Marques (1993) for a description of the accelerating invasion of Brazilians into neighboring Amazonian countries. Although gold prospectors appear to be the perpetrators of recent violence against native peoples within their reservations, these incidents are also indicative of intra-Amazonian migration pressures against boundaries of all kinds, be they international or protective of reserves.

17. Credit and fiscal incentives that increased the value of land and the ability of large farmers to buy out small ones may have accelerated this centuries-old process during the late 1970s and early 1980s.

CHAPTER 3

Economic Shifts in the Amazon during the 1980s

Since migratory patterns tend to reflect the nature of economic activity and trends, the boom of the 1970s and the crisis of the 1980s affected migratory movement in the Amazon differently. This chapter concentrates on the impact of the 1980s national economic crisis—the worst in Brazil's modern history—on the economic dynamics of the frontier. The chapter bears important results for the discussion of intraregional migratory movements found in the remaining chapters of the book.

The main finding is that general economic crisis and a weakening federal government are being countered in the Amazon by strengthening provincial governments and growing local economies. In response to generalized economic crisis, frontier agents are increasingly channeling resources to local real estate, provoking a speculative run on land. As land markets consolidate in what had been the frontier of the 1970s, the pioneers of that decade set out for new land, with very small return migration.

It is possible that if Brazil's economic instability were to end, the economic and population adjustments made in response to the crisis could endure. This holds important implications for the relationship between general economic crisis and Amazon deforestation.

Changing Economic Contexts

The 1980s crisis eventually dampened the trend of the previous two decades, marked by steadily increasing interregional migration. Among the numerous causes of this earlier (1960s and 1970s) geographic mobility were:

- A combination of legal, political, economic, and agricultural factors that pushed small farmers out of established farming areas of the South, Southeast, and Northeast. These included (a) legal and political changes in labor relations in agriculture (Mesquita and Silva 1987a); (b) a long peak in the business cycle (the "Brazilian miracle"), driving up real estate prices, mainly in the South, which in turn financed the spontaneous outmigration of southern family farmers (illustrated by Rezende 1981 and Brito 1987); (c) the penetration of the soybean crop in the South and Center-West, consolidating small holdings into large ones (Mesquita and Silva 1987b and c); and (d) a severe drought in the Northeast in the early 1970s, expelling the rural population from a vast area.

- A military dictatorship that promoted a policy of Amazonian occupation during a period of easy access to international finance for large-scale projects.[1] This regime, motivated by xenophobia, geopolitics, and development aspirations, catalyzed the forces that promoted occupation. Characterized by concentrated decisionmaking and executive power, the military government created vast resource-using projects in mining, smelting, hydroelectric power, and other industries, attracting to the Amazon hordes of workers and farmers from distant regions. Improvements in transport and telecommunications systems were made, facilitating long-distance, interregional migration; and the establishment of agricultural credit and fiscal incentives expanded agroindustrial and commercial agriculture in frontier areas. All of the above, together with official land titling and directed colonization programs, increased the accessibility of the Amazon to large and small farmers and to an increasing variety of agents. Ozório de Almeida (1991a and 1992) gives further information on this point.

Martine (1992a) and Sawyer (1990) describe how in the 1980s and early 1990s the forces that had earlier contributed to geographic mobility declined. Much of the migration-prone population of former share tenants, ex-*minifundiários*, and ex-squatters was gradually absorbed at the source, mostly by cities and towns (many as *bóias-frias*) and some by the frontier, reducing the pool of potential interregional migrants to the Amazon.

National Economic Context of the 1980s: Shifts in Fiscal Revenues

Federal authority for macroeconomic management in Brazil has experienced a profound transformation as a result of the institutional changes that culminated in the new federal constitution in October 1988. The constitution provided for greater decentralization of responsibilities, a considerable redistribution of revenues,[2] and an increase in the power of subnational governments.[3]

The Transition to Democracy and Fiscal Decentralization

The constitutional changes have had a somewhat greater impact in the frontier than in Brazil as a whole. Table 3.1 shows the geometric annual rates of growth of locally collected tax income, transfers, and current revenues in the states of Pará and Mato Grosso, as well as for the entire frontier (Amazon plus *cerrado*), and for Brazil as a whole.[4] The first two columns in each section of the table show two periods: 1982–88 and 1989–91. These are the pre- and post-constitutional reform periods, respectively. The third column in each section shows decade averages. Differentiating between the pre- and post-reform periods sheds light on more recent frontier trends, which otherwise would be lost in decade averages.

Column 3 of table 3.1 shows that the total annual tax income on the frontier grew at a much faster rate than in Brazil as a whole throughout the decade. This relatively high growth rate was not unusual, given the increasing urbanization (discussed in chapter 2) and the organization of a complex market network in the Amazon during the 1980s. This point will be discussed in detail in the section entitled "Amazonian Economic Context" (page 27). It is to be expected that the tax base would rise as established markets grow and that tax evasion would decrease as enforcement improves.

In the state of Pará (Eastern Amazonia), tax income over the decade grew at a faster rate than in Mato Grosso (Western Amazonia). This difference

Table 3.1 Geometric Average Annual Growth Rates of Tax Income, Transfers, and Current Revenues for Pará, Mato Grosso, and the North, 1982–91

	Tax income			Transfers			Current revenues		
	1	2	3	4	5	6	7	8	9
Location	1982–88	1989–91	1982–91	1982–88	1989–91	1982–91	1982–88	1989–91	1982–91
Pará (Eastern Amazonia)	3.46	30.51	11.79	4.41	29.27	12.19	3.89	30.00	11.95
Mato Grosso (Western Amazonia)	9.67	10.47	9.94	1.46	10.41	4.36	6.96	10.45	8.11
Total North[a]	7.10	27.21	13.42	6.10	17.60	9.81	6.49	21.57	11.29
Brazil	0.44	9.31	3.32	9.75	7.79	9.10	2.14	8.96	4.47

a. Comprises all frontier states, not only Mato Grosso and Pará. Thus, averages for total North are averages over all frontier states.

Source: Adapted from the SAFEM database. Based on constant 1991 cruzeiros.

is probably associated with the structure of commercial activities in each flank of the frontier. Eastern Amazonian colonization is relatively older than that of Western Amazonia, and those who migrated there during the 1970s were mostly poor Northeasterners who established a relatively atomized structure of commercial activities. Enforcement was loose in the region until the late 1980s, and taxation was relatively easy to avoid. For example, while the average annual growth rate of tax income in Pará was 3.46 percent from 1982–1988, it climbed to 30.51 percent after the 1988 reform. The state's increased monitoring responsibilities and improved enforcement, however, do not account fully for this dramatic increase in the rates of growth of tax income. As will be discussed later in this chapter, the growth of economic activity in the frontier and, consequently, the tax base, has contributed to the steep growth rate of tax income in the North. Unfortunately, the two events—improved enforcement and an increase in the tax base—are not separable in table 3.1.

Western Amazonia, in turn, is a younger frontier with a larger proportion of better-off migrants, most from the South and Southeast, the richest regions of Brazil. The type of economic activities conducted on this side of the Amazon contrast strongly with the atomized commercial structure of the East. Here, intense and highly structured trade with the South since the early days of occupation has resulted in larger and more visible establishments that could not as easily escape taxation. As a consequence, even with improved enforcement after constitutional reform, the growth rate of tax income over the decade was negligible, given the region's larger original base and type of economic activities (see first two columns in table 3.1).

Thus, the relatively high rates of growth in tax income on the frontier during the 1980s is apparently due to two events: an increase in the tax base as a result of local economic growth, especially in Eastern Amazonia, and improved enforcement, which reduced tax evasion.[5] This rapid growth shows an Amazon that is changing from being simply an alternative to penury for floating populations from outside the region, as it was in the 1970s, into a richer and more complex economy with a well-defined and fast-growing market structure.

Column 6 of table 3.1 shows that, over the decade, the frontier region kept pace with the rest of Brazil in terms of the rate of growth of transfers. However, after the 1988 constitutional reform, the rate of growth of transfers to Amazon states climbed dramatically, in contrast with the rest of Brazil. This recent increase in the amount of transfers from the federal government to the states of the North and Center-West has further strengthened the economy of the region.

Current revenues in both the Eastern and Western flanks of the Amazon grew at much faster rates than throughout the rest of Brazil during the 1989–91 period (see column 9). Such a growth rate was strikingly higher in the 1989–91 period than in the 1982–88 period. Five simultaneous trends have contributed to this growth: escalation of government transfers to frontier states; proliferation of tax legislation empowering state and local governments to increase their shares and incidence in old and new taxes; improvement in enforcement; increase in incomes derived from the operation and staffing of local and state agencies, as well as of NGOs and other institutions; and, finally, increase in the number and incomes of private initiatives, not only in farming, ranching, and commerce, but also in mining, processing, and other industries (see "The merchant frontier," page 27).

Growing local economic power is thus adding to increasing local political power (provided by democratization) in determining the use and distribution of local natural resources. Meanwhile, national-level political and economic powers are dwindling in the Amazon.

Reduction in fiscal and credit incentives

The recent growth of frontier economic activity and the constitutional reform of 1988 inserted the Amazon into the broader national economic context yet allowed the region to maintain its local dynamics. The fact that most strikingly distinguishes the Amazon of the 1970s from that of today is the capability to generate revenues locally, counterbalancing somewhat the loss of fiscal and credit incentives that occurred during the crisis of the 1980s.

Fiscal and credit incentives have been held responsible for much of the acquisition and deforestation of large tracts of land in the Amazon during the 1970s (Ozório de Almeida 1992). These incentives began to decline during the early 1980s, as can be seen in table 3.2, and subsidized rural credit in the 1990s is practically nonexistent.

During the 1970s, fiscal incentives augmented the demand for farm-, pasture-, and ranchland, thereby increasing deforestation on the frontier of settlement and accelerating the conversion of forest to farmland in already settled areas (Binswanger 1994 and chapter 5 this volume). The tax code, until recently, essentially exempted agriculture, converting it into a tax shelter. Since it was relatively easy to claim any frontier activity as agricultural in nature, this exemption contributed to the run on land by urban investors and corporations attempting to diversify their asset portfolios. Tax havens, together with credit subsidies, provoked an early boom in speculative demand for Amazonian land. Mahar (1989), Binswanger (1994), and Serôa da Motta 1991 treat this point.

In the 1990s, however, frontier agents can no longer exclude most of their agricultural profits from their taxable income.[6] This contributes to an increase in local tax revenues and empowers local governments to invest in local physical and social infrastructure. To a certain extent, new revenues are, therefore, compensating for lost subsidies.[7]

Table 3.2 Official Rural Credit in Classic Amazonia, 1970–85

Year	Amount (US$)	Year	Amount (US$)
1970	61,692	1978	775,219
1971	89,220	1979	1,062,085
1972	153,763	1980	1,095,666
1973	178,498	1981	748,273
1974	118,669	1982	506,628
1975	288,321	1983	275,168
1976	523,506	1984	115,352
1977	573,674	1985	172,795

Note: Average 1985 exchange rate: Cr$2,144/US$. Inflation in the United States from 1985 to 1991 = 24.78 percent (World Bank data).
Source: Adapted from Mahar 1989.

Reduction in other federal activities

The political transition to democracy and newly decentralized fiscal federalism dramatically weakened the decisionmaking power of the federal government. In addition, escalating external debt and deteriorating commodity prices made the government more vulnerable to those who opposed expanding the agricultural frontier. As pressures from international agencies and NGOs grew, the general public became more interested in, and informed about, Amazonian issues.

Dwindling federal budgets killed many federal infrastructure investments, while local urban centers, swelled by newly urbanized voters with political clout, increasingly defined local priorities. Political and economic opposition to large-scale federal projects, such as hydroelectric dams, grew while state and municipal projects multiplied.

Federal investments during the decade of colonization—road construction, titling, settlement, services—that had cost billions of dollars during the 1970s, fell drastically, further discouraging potential migrants during the 1980s (Sawyer 1990).[8] Although vast tracts of land continued to be auctioned off to private colonization firms, or to forestry–agroindustrial concerns from the South and from abroad, they were no longer outrageous giveaways as they had been during the heyday of land purchasing credit and other fiscal incentives (Ozório de Almeida 1991a). Some large-scale projects were initiated and/or continued during the 1980s in mining and smelting, hydroelectricity, and other industries, although these tended to have local impact only (the broadest, by far, being that of Carajás) and to attract migrants from adjacent areas.[9]

Summary

As the national economic crisis dragged on throughout the 1980s, the forces that had promoted interregional mobility during the 1970s weakened, while new ones emerged that may have reduced interregional mobility even further. Among these new forces were the transition to democracy, the newly decentralized fiscal federalism, a sharp decline in fiscal and rural credit incentives, and a reduction of public expenditures on infrastructure.

Probably the effects of these changes will be enduring. Even if national priorities were to shift back toward deliberate inducements to settle in the Amazon, Brazilian society has learned over the past two decades that farming the Amazon is an arduous undertaking, that risks are high, and that many have failed. The economic and demographic forces of the 1980s were such that an increase in interregional migration is highly improbable.

Despite the strong reduction in credit and fiscal incentives to agriculture, and reductions in other federal initiatives in the Amazon, forest clearing did not correspondingly decline during the late 1980s. This suggests that Amazonian deforestation during this period responded to intra-frontier forces different from those of the 1970s or even those of the early or mid-1980s. Although the speculative motive for deforestation may have begun with incentives from the federal government, it is now being fed by local stimuli.

Amazonian Economic Context: Shifts in Economic Activities

Merchants comprise a large segment of the new frontier's urban middle class. The remainder of this chapter will discuss the emergence and economic evolution of these frontier merchants and the implications of their economic behavior for small-farmer intraregional migration and deforestation.[10] Because of space limitations, it has not been possible to deal with all members of the Amazon's rising and highly diversified urban middle class, including persons associated with mining, hydroelectricity, manufacturing, processing, and other sectors, or with governmental agencies and NGOs active in Amazonian affairs.

The merchant frontier

Although the Amazon is typically thought of as an agricultural frontier, it has always been more urban than rural, due to the staffing of local public sector agencies and the growth of local commercial activity (Ozório de Almeida 1992). The precocious urbanization of the frontier, discussed in the previous chapter, is not solely demographic.[11] An economic dimension of urbanization lies in the presence of a diversified and voluminous tertiary sector: commerce, services, and the public sector. Although many urban services, especially personal services, are undoubtedly swelled by the disguised unemployment of former farmers expelled from the land, frontier commerce is nonetheless highly profitable with outstanding rates of accumulation (Hébette and Marin 1977).

The importance of local merchants can hardly be overemphasized in a discussion of the recent expansion of the Amazonian frontier. These economic agents practice a varied set of activities, all of which have some role in linking primary frontier activities—farming and extraction—to the rest of the economy through market transactions for agricultural or extractive products, productive inputs, consumer goods, credit, land, and labor. (For a detailed discussion of market transactions between merchants and farmers, see Ozório de Almeida 1992.)

These local transactions determine the appropriation of income and the rate of return both of primary producers—farmers and extractivists—and of merchants. Rates that are above opportunity costs for merchants should invite new entries. However, distance, lack of communications, high transport costs, and other factors may constitute barriers to such entries and foster natural monopolies among merchants, especially when a frontier is relatively new. Such local monopolies may, in turn, reduce prices paid (or increase prices charged) to farmers and reduce farmers' incomes.[12] According to standard long-run microeconomic analysis, rates to return in a given market signal entries, exits, or stability in that market. But in a frontier, where markets are still incipient, the rates of return to merchants become important also in determining entries, exits, or stability among local small farmers. Whether a frontier consolidates with its pioneering small farmers, or whether pioneers are expelled by newcomers and by land concentration, depends greatly on the operation of frontier markets and their merchants.[13]

Merchant accumulation by type of activity

The merchant frontier seems to lag behind the farming frontier.[14] In the 1970s, businesses in frontier towns were mainly associated with primary activities.[15] This pattern, however, changed in the course of the 1980s, yielding a spectrum of tertiary sector activities with very high rates of accumulation of physical and financial assets.[16]

Overall, the monthly average rate of accumulation of frontier merchants in 1991 was an impressive 2.56 percent (see table 3.3 and various tables from Penalva Santos 1993).[17] This was in fact low when compared to the average of 14.5 percent ten years earlier.[18] What had been beginners' monopoly power apparently eroded during the 1980s, as new entrants competed for local markets, as the towns themselves grew and diversified, and as local

Table 3.3 Monthly Rates of Accumulation by Type of Operation, 1991

Type of operation	Eastern Amazonia	Western Amazonia	Frontier total
Sawmills	—	0.94	0.94
Merchants of agricultural products	4.62	2.23	3.55
Suppliers of agricultural inputs	1.82	2.88	2.31
Suppliers of consumption goods	0.42	2.76	1.63
Others	3.92	3.38	3.48
Total	2.44	2.65	2.56

— Not available.
Note: The figures above are weighted averages, based on the number of people interviewed.
Source: Penalva Santos 1993.

agricultural lands were increasingly turned to pasture (Mattos, Uhl, and Goncalves 1992).

The poor performance of sawmills in comparison with most other merchant activities by the early 1990s was apparently caused by the migration of loggers and mills out of old frontiers and on to new ones, as unsustainable tree harvesting eradicated valuable species.[19]

Sawmills aside, Western Amazonia appears to have had a more homogeneous merchant economy, exhibiting smaller differences in accumulation rates among different types of merchants, than did Eastern Amazonia. This may be due to strong links to a more homogeneous set of trading partners in the South. The lowest accumulation rates were among merchants of agricultural products (purchasers, transporters, and processors), partly caused by the decline of agriculture and the spread of pastures in much of the old frontier of Western Amazonia. The highest accumulation rates in this region were not sustained by outside markets but by growing local urban economies served by other business activities (see *Others* in table 3.3). This category includes bars, pool and gambling houses, hotels, brothels, restaurants, dentists, doctors, hairdressers, barbers, and others.

In Eastern Amazonia, accumulation rates varied more widely among merchant types, with outstandingly high ones for merchants of agricultural products, followed by local commerce.[20] This indicates an agricultural economy strong enough to sustain such merchants, possibly due to the maturing of perennials, such as cocoa, pepper, and even sugarcane. Also, long-term, historical, river-based trading monopolies initiated by extractivist merchants may be moving into expanding agricultural product markets and imposing their traditional monopoly power over farmers.

Suppliers of industrialized agricultural inputs (equipment, fertilizers, pesticides, mechanical components, and repairs) had higher rates of accumulation—suggesting more industrialized agriculture—in the Western than in the Eastern Amazon. Interestingly, overall, agriculture-related merchants fared better than vendors of consumer goods (pharmacies, groceries, clothing, and odds and ends).

Thus, during the 1980s in old Amazonian frontiers, merchants' accumulation rates decreased, their monopoly power over farmers diminished, and thriving urban businesses grew. The most successful among the merchants were those who continued to function as intermediaries in frontier commerce, linking local farmers to the rest of the economy.

Merchant accumulation by market range

The geographic market range of merchant activity indicates the main regions to which Amazon frontier transactions were being channeled. Table 3.4 displays accumulation data from different Amazonian regional markets. Variations in accumulation rates were higher in Eastern than in Western Amazonia. Western Amazonia sold predominantly to the South (in this case including the Southeast), while Eastern Amazonia sold to the South and the North (in this case including the Northeast).[21] The highest accumulation rates were among local-North merchants in Eastern Amazonia, who bought goods from local suppliers (mainly farmers) and sold them to northern clients.[22]

The data do not show the incidence of merchants in Eastern Amazonia purchasing from northern suppliers, but rather from the South and Center (the latter usually relaying southern-produced goods transported through the Center). In general, merchants who brought outside (mainly manufactured) goods to the frontier had much lower accumulation rates than those who took goods from the frontier to the outside economy. This may be a reflection of the undervaluing of the region's natural resources, where low land values and relatively open access drive user costs downward.

Western Amazonia attracted a far higher proportion of southern migrants than did Eastern Amazonia, and southern migrants tended to be better off than other migrants, who were mostly northeasterners (Ozório de Almeida 1992). As indicated in table 3.4, Western communities tended to be more prosperous than Eastern ones, and local-local merchants appear to have had somewhat higher accumulation rates in Western than Eastern Amazonia.

Western Amazonia's markets were more interactive than those of Eastern Amazonia, in the sense that they supplied frontier products to, and consumed industrialized goods from, the South. There were more barriers to entry in commerce in Western Amazonia, which is consistent with the fact that suppliers of industrialized inputs and consumer goods had higher rates of accumulation in the West than in the East (Ozório de Almeida 1992). In fact, most frontier businesses in Western Amazonia today are run by southerners, who were encouraged to come to the frontier by the private

Table 3.4 Accumulation by Range of Markets, 1991

Range of markets (supplier-consumer)	Eastern Amazonia	Western Amazonia	Frontier total
Local-local	1.95	3.42	2.42
Local-North	10.65	—	10.65
Local-Center	—	—	—
Local-South	3.33	3.03	3.08
North-local	—	1.45	1.45
Center-local	1.28	1.00	1.20
South-local	1.86	2.17	2.09
Total	2.44	2.65	2.56

— Not available.
Note: The figures above are weighted averages, based on the number of people interviewed.
Source: Penalva Santos 1993.

colonization programs of the 1970s. Industrial headquarters in the South financed the establishment of frontier branches, or established regular supply contracts (for example, mechanical parts, components, and so forth, for direct sale or repair services) with local businesses, with an eye to increasing earnings and future remittances back to the firms of origin.[23] Unfortunately, space limitations prevent further examination of the development of traditional mercantile colonization or of interregional imperialism in the Brazilian Amazon.

Commercial profits not sent to trading partners outside the Amazon tend to be invested in local land purchases, mostly by southern merchants, as discussed below.

Merchant accumulation in land

Two different activities in which frontier merchants accumulate are commerce and agriculture. Many of those who migrated to the Amazon did so because they wanted to become landowners, and commerce may have been a stepping-stone to that end.[24] In 1991 agricultural assets represented almost one-third of merchants' total assets (32.13 percent as a weighted average). The highest average is in Western Amazonia, where 33.32 percent of total merchant assets are agricultural. This weighted average indicates that western (originally southern) merchants invested proportionately more in land than did eastern (mostly originally northeastern) merchants (28.87 percent) (Penavla Santos 1993).

In a frontier, becoming a commercial farmer or rancher requires investments with long gestation periods. Gaining title to land implies mapping, demarcating, litigating, and registering the plot with different, loosely coordinated official entities and authorities, who must be present for contracts to be enforceable. Surveying, forest cutting, burning, stumpage, and soil correction must all be done before ordinary farming or ranching begin, and markets for credit, agricultural products, inputs, and labor must be established for commercial farming to be able to operate. Since commercial farming cannot function outside the standard institutions of a market economy—with local wage-labor scarcity posing a potential problem for those who intend to engage in such activity in new frontiers—many migrants tend first to operate urban businesses and only slowly, over the years, to invest in agriculture.[25] The consolidation and concentration of land ownership, the occurrence of rural exodus and urbanization, and the formation of a wage-based labor force all contribute to easing the way for local commercial agriculture to develop.[26] Until this becomes possible, merchants bide their time purchasing land. Whether they will eventually become productive commercial farmers or hold the land for speculative purposes will depend on relative returns.

Of course, Amazonian reality is far more complex and varied than would appear from such a schematic rendering. In many locations, commercial farming precedes and preempts small farmer settlements. In others, there is no attempt to farm whatsoever; only ranching or outright speculative landgrabbing exists.

What is clear is that in old frontiers during the inflationary economy of the 1980s, merchant demand for land for speculative rather than for productive purposes increased.[27] In general, the land these merchants bought was sold to them by poor (although not exclusively so) local farmers, who moved on to deforest farther inland. Without agricultural experience or expertise, such new urbanite landowners have tended to eradicate crops, even productive perennials such as coffee and cocoa, and turned much of the land to pasture.[28] The next chapter provides field data on these trends.

Summary and Policy Implications: Shifts in Public and Private Resources

The crisis of the 1980s brought changes to both the overall Brazilian economy and that of the Amazonian frontier. Factors such as federal fiscal subsidies and credit, as well as expenditures on colonization, land titling, and roads that had promoted interregional migration throughout the 1970s began to disappear in the 1980s. Meanwhile, the transition to democracy, increasingly decentralized fiscal federalism, and a growing urban economy promoted intraregional migration. A frontier middle class, composed of merchants and other groups, such as public servants, private sector employees, and others, is becoming the ultimate beneficiary of deforestation in the Amazon.

Markets for land, labor credit, consumer goods, and agricultural inputs and products have favored the development of urban private businesses. As landownership has consolidated in areas that had been new frontiers in the 1970s, commercial agriculture and commercial urban activity have grown. These old frontiers are linked to the rest of the Brazilian economy by merchants who transact with local farmers and extractivists, a role that appears to profit both the merchants and their outside trading partners. The number of agents interested in, and actively involved with, the growth of the Amazonian economy is far greater than those actually living in the region. Thus, economic policies that alter frontier trends will affect a large and growing business community, inside and outside the Amazon.

The growing urban economy of the Amazon is not leading to sustainability for small farmers. Whether in response to inflation and the protracted national economic crisis, or for the sake of speculative gains as land markets consolidate, the urban middle class is purchasing more and more land. This further inflates frontier land prices, pushes pioneer farmers out, stimulates intra-regional migration, and causes the spread of unfarmed, deforested land. Any policies aimed at curbing deforestation must take into account who these newcomers are and what their motives are for holding land.

Notes

1. A detailed treatment of these issues goes beyond the scope of this book. Due to the complexity of the discussion and the abundant existing literature, only major references are provided.

2. The 1988 constitution provided for a considerable redistribution of revenues via an increased role for state and municipal participation funds—unconditional bloc transfers that had both a decentralizing and redistributive role. Socolik (1989), for example, argues that in 1988 the municipal participation fund (Fundo de Participacao dos Municipios—FPM) represented some 50 percent of current revenues of municipalities in most cities of the North, as opposed to 25 percent of revenues of cities in other regions of Brazil. At the regional level, in 1991 transfers represented 55 percent of current revenues in the North and 37.5 percent in the Center-West (SAFEM database). See Bonfim and Shah (1991), Serra and Afonso (1993, page 35), and Shah (1990) on the distributive effect of transfers on each level of government.

3. See Shah (1990) and Bonfim and Shah (1991) for a discussion on the specific changes brought about by the new constitution.

4. Note that for this table, data for the entire frontier had to be used (Amazon plus *cerrado*), rather than for just the Amazon frontier, or the North region, because of shifts in data collection units during the 1980s. Regional trends in the North cannot be consistently observed during this time because two federal territories in the region graduated into the category of states, beginning to collect taxes only when the decade was already well under way (as opposed to the other states of the North). This fact would tend to overemphasize the regional growth rates of tax income in the later years of the decade. Furthermore, a relatively rich new state, Tocantins,

was created and transferred from the Center-West to the North, after Goias was divided; this would also tend to overemphasize the growth rates in the North. The states of Pará and Mato Grosso have been singled out in the table because they have the highest figures in the region, avoid the redefinitional problems just cited, are representative of the Eastern and Western Amazonian frontiers in general, and are the locations of the field surveys discussed in chapter 3 and analyzed in chapters 4, 5, and 6.

5. Aside from improved enforcement, a large variety of tax instruments began to accrue to state and local governments directly, due to the tax reforms of the 1980s, such as value added tax and service tax. This also increased local tax income.

6. Although the extinction of tax havens that had promoted deforestation did actually reduce the rate at which the Amazon was being deforested by the late 1980s, *that part of deforestation caused by small farmers increased considerably*. This issue will be treated in detail in chapter 5.

7. For example, according to table 3.1, total official rural credit to Classic Amazonia amounted to almost US$1.1 million in 1980, its largest year. By 1982 rural credit had already begun to decline, reaching US$506,600. Meanwhile, fiscal revenues for the region were already much larger, US$360 million (SAFEM data, using 1991 constant cruzeiros and exchange rate of Cr$963.80/US$). A decade later, in 1991, total fiscal revenues were US$1.1 billion, which is a thousand times the value of subsidized credit at its height in 1980. This calculation does not take into account the amount of income brought into the Amazon via tax subsidies and shelters. The consensus in the literature, however, appears to be that the rate of return on such subsidized projects was negative and that very little was gained by them in the region. See Ozório de Almeida (1991a) for a discussion of this literature.

8. See Ozório de Almeida (1992, chapters 6 through 10) for detailed costs of colonization during the 1970s. On average, federal expenditures were approximately US$750,000 per year. This is more than subsidized credit, except for the peak four years of 1978–81, according to table 3.2. The demise of the federal colonization program was, thus, a significant additional loss in federal resources to the Amazon. It is not yet clear how much state settlement programs compensated for this loss during the 1980s. Also see Sawyer (1990).

9. See Ozório de Almeida (1991a) for a partial listing of economic agents active in the Amazon during the 1980s.

10. This and the following sections draw extensively on Penalva Santos (1993), which was based on field research undertaken by the Institute of Applied Economic Research (IPEA) of the Brazilian Ministry of Economics and Finance in 1991 under the project Colonização Sustentável na Amazônia. (The box in chapter 4 gives a detailed description of the field survey.) Results for 1991 have sometimes been compared to those of a 1981 field survey held in the same Amazonian locations, as presented in Ozório de Almeida (1992, chapter 15).

11. Precocious in terms of population density in the Northern region.

12. When the frontiers of the 1970s were new, merchants' monopoly power was indeed compressing farmers' incomes, especially in Western Amazônia, as shown in Ozório de Almeida (1992, chapters 15 and 18).

13. Chapters 4 and 5 will specify in detail the relationship between rates of remuneration of (and opportunity costs to) productive factors—land, labor, capital—and the sustainability of small farmers, as measured by turnover and deforesta-

tion. The remaining sections of this chapter merely describe the economic conditions, as viewed through merchants' perspectives, that bring forth those rates and costs for farmers.

Schmink and Wood (1992) discuss the historical evolving role of Amazonian elites and merchants, focusing on their sociopolitical dynamics at the local, state, and national levels. See also Browder (1988).

14. What had been the new frontiers (absorbers of net migratory inflows) of the 1970s became the old frontiers (expellers of net migratory outflows) of the 1980s. Nowadays the old frontier is itself inside the Amazon. The term "old frontier" refers to the areas where the inflow of small farmers was greatest during the early 1970s, and where their expulsion was also greatest during the 1980s, according to the maps in chapter 2.

15. The feverish road building of the 1970s brought on farming and ranching, cleared accessible land of forests, and displaced, sometimes violently, traditional forest extraction (rubber tapping, nut gathering, logging, and so forth), which had been based on river transport. This changed the structure of Amazonian urban commerce, as will be seen in table 3.3.

Roads also facilitated the invasion of prospectors. This was especially unfortunate for the environment, as prospecting, especially for gold, is one of the worst polluters in the Amazon, destroying immense river basins with mercury and other hazards. Prospecting was very favorable to commerce, however. In many road-frontier towns of the 1970s, prospecting sustained urban commerce until farming, ranching, and logging started to pay off. Unfortunately, the authors were unable to interview any prospectors, who are secretive about their affairs.

16. The rate of accumulation measures the rate of increase in real net worth over time, that is, the geometric average rate of increase in real value of physical and financial assets minus debt outstanding from the time of arrival at the frontier to the present. In cross-sections it is a better measurement of performance over time than the rate of return, which requires observations of an income stream at several different moments in time. By disregarding all incomes not reinvested in the business, the rate of accumulation can be considered an underestimate of the rate of return.

17. Frontier commerce is extremely diversified, and all merchants transact in a broad range of markets. In fact, market interlinking is a notorious feature of frontiers, whereby one agent concentrates several market functions, such as in the case of debt peonage, when credit-product-labor markets are interlinked. The data in table 3.3 refer to the dominant, though not necessarily (in fact rarely) exclusive, type of operation of merchants.

18. See Ozório de Almeida (1992, table 32). These outstanding rates of accumulation in some frontier locations in the early days did not last long and soon lowered to the standard shown in table 3.3 and in appendix A, table A.4.

19. See Ozório de Almeida (1992, chapter 15). See also Uhl and others (1991) for insightful discussions of logging activities in the Amazon. The locations from which these data are drawn are described in the box in chapter 4.

According to Zweede (1993), newer loggers and mills associated with the farming frontier migrated after the farmers, along the new highways, toward areas where the forest was being cleared for agriculture or ranching. Older loggers and mills, associated with traditional riverside extractivism, did not move with the farmers and remained where they were, harvesting increasingly lower-grade trees.

20. See the box in chapter 4 for a description of surveyed communities.

21. Merchants in all parts of the Amazon frontier were in fact trading with partners all over Brazil. The data refer only to the dominant, but not necessarily (in fact rarely) exclusive, trading partners of the frontier merchants interviewed. Trade between the Amazon frontier and the Center-West is well-known, but it is hidden (table 3.4) by the dominant influences of the South and the North.

22. It is interesting to observe that this route follows, by road, the traditional commercial river transport ties of Amazonian extractivism to exporters and processors in Santarém and Belém.

23. See merchant company histories based on field interviews in 1991 in Penalva Santos (1993).

24. See Ozório de Almeida (1992, chapters 12 and 15) for a discussion of the interaction between merchants and farmers during different stages of frontier settlement.

25. Numerous efforts are traditionally made to circumvent the labor scarcity problem of the Brazilian Center-West and North regions. These often involve recruiting and transporting workers from impoverished communities, generally in the Northeast; obligating them to a wide variety of debt peonage systems; and establishing some form of violent coercion or enslavement. In 1981, one of the authors witnessed large truck convoys illegally transporting cargoes of indebted peons to commercial farms along the Trans-Amazonian highway. The practice seems to have become even more widespread during the 1980s. See Ozório de Almeida (1991b) and Romanoff (1992).

26. See Ozório de Almeida (1992, chapters 12 and 15) for a more thorough discussion of frontier stages and merchant-farmer interactions.

27. Merchants' speculative demand for land will be seen to be a very important factor in undermining small farmer unsustainability in the Amazon, as will be discussed in chapters 4 and 5.

28. Thus, contrary to the usual emphasis of environmental economics, the issue is not property rights, or the lack thereof, but what causes property rights to become increasingly concentrated. The social and economic issues that provoked such concentration in former frontiers appear to be the main causes of Amazonian deforestation today.

CHAPTER 4

Land Markets and Sustainable Frontier Farming

In the 1980s a complex urban economy, commercially linked to the rest of the country, replaced the isolation of pioneer frontiers in the Amazon, with harsh consequences for small farmers and the forest. During this time the sustainability of small farmer settlements declined all over the frontier, as measured by changes in the ratio of private benefits to environmental costs. In low productivity frontiers, sustainability declined because benefits from settlement declined, given stable environmental costs. In high productivity frontiers, benefits from settlement remained stable, but environmental costs increased.

The evolution of farming in the 1980s varies widely throughout the Amazon in terms of crops, migrant origins, soil quality, physical and institutional infrastructure, and other characteristics. This chapter analyzes a representative sample of old Amazon frontiers, described in detail in the box (next page) and map 4.1. The authors recognize, however, that the basin is so diverse that no single sample can ever do it justice.

While only directed colonization projects, not spontaneous colonization frontiers, are included, many of the migrants interviewed were not settled in their plots by colonizing agencies, whether official or private.[1] Many squatted on the land for many years before acquiring claim to it, a frequent occurrence in official projects during the 1970s and early 1980s. Others purchased the land from earlier colonizers who left, a practice that became increasingly common in both spontaneous and directed colonization projects in the 1980s. In fact, the difference between the two types of colonization became more and more blurred as land turned increasingly into private property and the real estate market grew throughout the frontier.

Undoubtedly, however, the migrants sampled here—by being in directed colonization projects—benefitted from greater security of tenure and protection from violent social conflict than did most spontaneous migrants.[2] To the extent that personal and tenure security contributes to successful farming, colonists in these projects had an advantage over those in areas of

37

Map 4.1

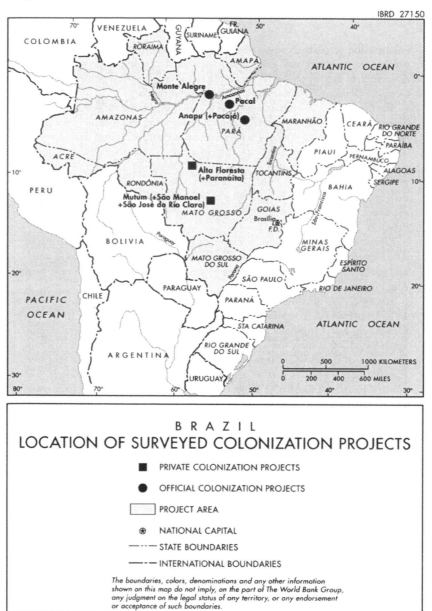

BRAZIL

LOCATION OF SURVEYED COLONIZATION PROJECTS

■ PRIVATE COLONIZATION PROJECTS

● OFFICIAL COLONIZATION PROJECTS

☐ PROJECT AREA

⊛ NATIONAL CAPITAL

—·—·— STATE BOUNDARIES

—·—·— INTERNATIONAL BOUNDARIES

The boundaries, colors, denominations and any other information shown on this map do not imply, on the part of The World Bank Group, any judgment on the legal status of any territory, or any endorsement or acceptance of such boundaries.

NOVEMBER 1995

Source: Ozório de Almeida (1992).

spontaneous settlement.[3] In this sense, then, the sample may consist of the elite of frontier migrants. If small farming turns out to be more successful in directed colonization projects than in the Amazon as a whole, then one should consider expanding those aspects of directed settlement that contribute to such successes. The objective of this chapter is to identify some of the most important determinants of diverse frontier outcomes and to isolate those that most contribute to sustainable frontier farming, specifically, those that decrease farmer turnover on plots.

Appendix A presents the descriptive tables discussed throughout the analysis in this chapter. The meaning and precise definition of each variable, a description of the sample, and a discussion of all empirical procedures used to construct the tables are presented in appendix B.)

Main Findings

During the 1980s, frontier farming apparently covered its opportunity costs in the labor and financial markets, but not in the land market. Earnings were high for family labor and for family assets, compared to the overall economy, making it worthwhile to continue farming in the frontier. Returns to land, however, were apparently low compared to rapidly appreciating frontier real estate, and farmers were motivated to move on and to reap capital gains successively from each plot of land. Settling a frontier, therefore, requires that land productivity keep up with land prices. Where this occurred, turnover on lots was low and settlement was relatively successful.

High productivity farming, however, turns out to be associated not only with high retention rates (low turnover) of farmers on the land, but also with high rates of deforestation on already occupied plots. Thus, while high productivity farming indirectly prevents the deforestation of new plots farther inland, it promotes greater levels of deforestation directly on the occupied plots. In order to escape this paradox, one must first analyze how deforestation rates respond to farm productivity and then devise appropriate economic policies to reduce "productive deforestation." The rapidity of turnover and deforestation, as discussed in the present chapter, spurs a renewed sense of urgency in the search for policies to curb the frontier advance in the Amazon.

Methodological Issues: Costs, Benefits, and Sustainability

This study attempts to take as much real world variation into account as possible in explaining the performance of small farmers in the Amazon and identify those policies that could increase the sustainability of frontier small farming. Given the variety of conditions in the Amazon, the evaluation of performance, based on the calculation of benefits and costs, is perhaps as important as the conceptual framework of analysis, that is, how these costs and benefits are defined, measured, and analyzed.

Benefits of settlement

In order to derive private benefits from settling the frontier, farmers must cover their opportunity costs in some or all factor markets: labor, capital, and land. These opportunity costs are calculated as follows:

- *Labor market.* As half the Brazilian urban labor force earns less than a minimum wage (in real terms, approximately US$1,000 per year, varying with the annual inflation rate), the minimum wage is a reasonable upper-bound proxy for small farmers' opportunity costs in this market.[4] In these terms, small farmers cover such opportunity costs if family labor income is at least one minimum wage per worker.
- *Capital market.* The only financial instrument widely available to small savers is the savings certificate (*caderneta de poupança*), which paid in 1991 a real interest rate of 0.5 percent per month. If this is used as a proxy for opportunity costs in the capital market, then small farmers cover these opportunity costs if the accumulation rate of all physical and financial assets is at least 0.5 percent per month.[5]
- *Land market.* The price per hectare of land is a straightforward variable. Farmers cover opportunity costs in this market if the rate of return to the use of the land is at least equal to the percentage variation in the price of the land during the same period.[6]

As long as real wage rates in the economy as a whole are low compared to real earnings on the frontier, and accumulation rates for small capital in the informal sector of the economy are low relative to those of frontier farmers, then Amazon settlers will cover their opportunity costs in the labor and capital markets.[7] On the other hand, as long as speculative demand for land hikes up real estate prices, then Amazon settlers will tend *not* to cover their opportunity costs in the land market.

The private benefits of settlement increase as the private returns to labor, capital, and land rise and as the settler retention rate rises (that is, turnover on lots falls). The longer settlers remain on their plots, the longer they will accrue benefits. Thus, policies that increase farm incomes and reduce turnover should increase the benefits of frontier small farming.[8]

Costs of settlement

In broad terms, the total costs of settlement include both private and environmental costs. Private costs comprise current and start-up costs, which include conventional fixed costs plus the farm-level costs of deforestation. Relatively open-access frontier conditions tend to reduce these costs, as access to forested land tends to be cheap relative to established areas. Other private costs of settlement are related to uncertainty and lack of information, which introduce considerable variance into expected returns on any one piece of land.

Environmental costs arise with improper farming and mismanagement of nonrenewable natural resources. These costs include, among others, the loss of biodiversity and the erosion of soil. Although it is difficult to measure environmental costs, one can identify conditions in which they are reduced.[9] For example, cost reductions occur per unit of benefit when, for any given deforested area, agricultural intensity increases, such as when crop yields rise, the ratio of harvested to total cleared area rises, or the number of harvests rises prior to turning land to pasture or fallow.

Very often there is an interplay between low private and high environmental costs. By providing cheap access to forested lands, frontier open-access conditions induce a wasteful use of soils (many times cleared for extensive agriculture and ranching), increasing the environmental costs of settlement.

Sustainability

Amazon farming will probably never be sustainable in the sense that it can fully replace all of the natural resources it uses. However hard to define and measure sustainability, when the ratio of private benefits to environmental costs rises, one could say that there has been an increase in sustainability.[10] Using this notion, sustainability can be increased in tropical farming by:

(1) reducing the environmental cost per unit of private benefit, for example, by decreasing the turnover or increasing farm income per hectare of deforested land;
(2) increasing the private costs of environmental destruction, for example, by internalizing the social cost of deforestation; and
(3) decreasing the private cost of alternatives that would cause less environmental damage, such as alternative tropical farming technologies.

Turnover on Frontier Plots

Overall, 64 percent of those interviewed in 1991 had been on the same lots in 1981, but this percentage varied widely across subgroups[11] (see appendix table A.1). Retention rates were higher in official colonization (67 percent) than in private colonization (61 percent). Within official colonization, it was higher among southerners (82 percent) than among other migrants (61 percent). Aside from Monte Alegre (81 percent), which is already in its third generation of colonists, the highest rate in Pará was in Pacal (74 percent), and in Mato Grosso, the highest rate was in Mutum (68 percent). The lowest rate was among other migrants in Pacajá (48 percent), located close to Pacal via the Trans-Amazonian Highway.

Opportunity Costs of Frontier Farming

In light of the variations in retention rates on lots, the following sections will investigate how economic alternatives compared with the opportunity costs of frontier farming.

Wage rate

In each survey, the opportunity cost in the labor market was taken to be the minimum wage (MW), US$1,000 per year. As mentioned previously, since roughly half the urban labor force in Brazil earns less than this, a lower value might provide a better comparison. Nonetheless, the minimum wage is the most widely accepted standard in Brazil and was therefore adopted here.

Payments to family labor can be approximated by measuring the value of monetary and nonmonetary yearly consumption per household and dividing this figure by the number of full-time adult workers.[12] The result is an estimate of how much families were remunerating their own labor and can be compared to the going wage in the labor market.

On average, there appears to have been a large increase in imputed remuneration to family labor over the 1980s, from 1.1 MW in 1981 to 3.2 MW in 1991 (table A.2). This increase seems to have been largest for southerners and those in private colonization projects. The imputed wage is significantly higher in Pacal (4.01 MW) and in Mutum (19.54 MW).

The dollar value of the imputed wage also grew (table A.2). Throughout the 1980s, exchange rate devaluation was smaller than the loss in real value of the minimum wage, so the change from 1981–91 is smaller in table A.3 than in table A.2. Differences among locations remain roughly the same. In this case, only Mutum, with its outstanding value (US$19,000), differed significantly from the rest.

On the average, family workers earned around US$4,000 per year, approximately US$333 per month, which is about four times the yearly minimum wage.[13] Even those in the lowest income groups self-remunerated above the minimum wage, albeit narrowly so. Note in table A.1 for example, the "Others" in Monte Alegre, as well as those in the highest turnover locations, São José do Rio Claro and Anapu-Pacajá. Thus, although much of the sample was very poor by international standards, it did better than average by domestic standards, given stringent conditions in the Brazilian labor market.[14] Using this criterion, therefore, frontier farming covered its opportunity costs in the labor market.

Interest rate

In the financial market, the opportunity cost of frontier farming is equivalent to the interest rate paid on the most widespread saving instrument for small and medium savers in Brazil, the *caderneta de poupança*. In 1991 this certificate paid 0.5 percent per month plus monetary correction.

The rate of accumulation is the average monthly percentage increase in net worth since arrival on the lot. It is measured by comparing all real and financial resources brought to the frontier with the value of net worth in 1991.[15] This concept is different from that of rate of return, which shows how much net income was earned on farmers' real assets over time. The accumulation rate is an alternative measure of asset appreciation.[16]

Appendix table A.4 shows that the average monthly real rate of accumulation was very high, about 2.3 percent, or more than four times the interest rate. Mutum, once again, had the highest figures. Although there were slight variations across locations and across migrant groups, these were statistically insignificant and small compared to variations in imputed wages.

The rate of accumulation, as measured, does not imply net additions to productive capacity, but merely additions to net asset values. Land is an important part of farmers' net worth (about 50 percent, on average), and rising land prices have contributed in a large measure to land appreciation (approximately 80 percent, on average). So capital gains have inflated accumulation rates by approximately 30 percent,[17] meaning real rates of accumulation were around 30 percent lower than those shown in table A.4. Even so, these real rates would still be at least double the interest rate. Farming, therefore, was very good business all over the frontier and covered its opportunity cost in the financial market.

Price of land

In the land market, the opportunity cost of land is the price of land per hectare.[18] This can be measured by weighting the microregional prices of forested areas, permanent or temporary crop areas, pasture areas, and fallow areas by the number of hectares devoted to each of these uses. Subsequently dividing the result by total land area gives one overall land price per plot.[19] This is the value the farmer would get by selling land under current market conditions. In this way, the change over time in the price of land can be compared to the rate of return gained from farming it.[20]

During the 1980s, the price of land rose considerably in most of the frontier. As we have seen, tax and credit incentives, large-scale colonization and titling programs, the laying down of physical and social infrastructure, and an inflationary economy all boosted demand for frontier land.[21] As people moved into the region, and more and more land became private property, the frontier land market began to operate dynamically, and real estate appreciated far more here than in the rest of the economy.[22]

According to calculations based on table A.8, during the 1980s average land prices seem to have appreciated much more in the public colonization projects of Pará (5.1 percent per year) than in the private ones of Mato

Grosso (1.4 percent). The highest rate of increase was in Anapu-Pacajá (11.1 percent), where land prices had been the lowest. The next highest were Pacal (6.6 percent) in the state of Pará and Mutum (6.1 percent) in the state of Mato Grosso. In Alta Floresta–Paranaíta, however, land values declined (–6.0 percent).

Across locations, land prices followed no trends. They sometimes rose with agricultural productivity, as in Mutum and Pacal, but they could appreciate despite declining productivity, as in Anapu-Pacajá. Neither did land prices necessarily reflect the amount or quality of infrastructure or government services available. Alta Floresta, known as the jewel of colonization and rated highest for physical and social infrastructure among all surveyed locations, witnessed declining land prices. Anapu-Pacajá, one of the most neglected areas along the Trans-Amazonian highway, saw sharply rising land prices. It appears, therefore, that exogenous factors contribute to variations in land prices in the Amazon frontier. Many determinants in widely varying weights are active in different places, and any generalizations would be simplistic.[23]

Land prices should be compared to the returns to land in agriculture in each location, to ascertain whether farmers are covering the opportunity cost of frontier farming in the land market. Unfortunately, it is difficult to measure the return to land, because factor remuneration is mixed with land rent. Open access conditions in a frontier further complicate the issue, as the price of land in relatively remote locations is, theoretically, zero (Campari 1993a and Deacon 1990). An added problem is that landed property rights have traditionally been poorly defined or enforced in the Amazon, with much of the basin having been exploited (under ambiguous titling concessions) by activities that were less focused on the land than on the forest covering it. This, of course, is the case in extraction, whether in forests (for example, rubber tapping, nut gathering, logging) or rivers (prospecting, fishing, and so forth). The patchwork effect of haphazard land titling has only confused matters even further, making it practically impossible to measure directly the real productive returns to land on the frontier. The next section, therefore, will look at indirect indicators of such returns.

Productivity, land use, and agricultural prices

The returns to land depend on the fertility of the soil, the intensiveness of land use, the productivity of other factors,[24] and prices of agricultural products.[25] See appendix tables A.5 to A.9. Total quantum productivity (table A.5) adds together kilograms of all crops and divides by harvested area. This, however, is flawed as an indicator of land productivity, because Pacal's extremely high productivity average, largely based on its production of sugarcane, an extremely bulky product, distorts total averages. The distribution of annual yields of rice, corn, and coffee (table A.7), however, indicates interesting productivity variations. Overall, productivity increased, with the greatest increases in Pacal (especially coffee) and Mutum, although there were some declines in Anapu-Pacajá and Alta Floresta–Paranaíta (rice). In several cases, considerable gains occurred over the ten-year period, even in temporary crops. Such gains may indicate that, as farmers gain experience, they learn to identify the best soil in their properties and acquire seeds and technologies most suitable for local conditions. Productivity gains are to be expected, of course, for perennial crops, such as coffee or cocoa, as trees mature. The significance of the general increase is considerable. It shows that contrary to widespread belief, productivity has *not* tended to decline in Amazonian soils.[26]

The average productivities of this group also compared well with national averages.[27] The few cases of constant or slightly declining productivities, such as in Alta Floresta–Paranaíta or Anapu-Pacajá, indicate involution from farming, eradication of perennials (mainly coffee in Alta Floresta), and the conversion of most of the deforested land to pastures. Elsewhere, as in Monte Alegre, slash-and-burn shifting agriculture left behind low productivity crops and expanding fallow areas to which farmers rarely, if ever, returned.

Table A.6 shows the low overall percentage of deforested land used for temporary and permanent crops (32.5 percent). In Pará, southerners were significantly more intensive farmers than others (36 percent compared with 26.9 percent). The highest intensity of land use for agriculture was in Mutum (84.7 percent), followed by Pacal (39.8 percent), with the lowest in Monte Alegre (18.4 percent), where many very old plots have already been totally deforested and abandoned by their owners.

Table A.8 indicates that agricultural prices during the 1980s were stagnant for basic temporary crops (rice and corn) and drastically declined for the main perennial (coffee). These figures are less than half those quoted at the international level, reflecting high transport costs to ports and to regional and national markets, as well as monopsonized frontier markets.[28]

Thus, during the 1980s, rates of return to land in the Amazon seem to have been rather poor in the face of strongly rising land prices. Agricultural prices were so low that, except for showcase locations, such as Pacal and Mutum, many farmers gave up on agriculture, sold their land, reaped capital gains, and moved on. Some went to other frontiers; others went to urban centers, where they set themselves up in business with the proceeds of their land sales. In fact, many of the most successful colonists in the sample had done exactly the same in the past. They had moved from frontier to frontier, as had their fathers and grandfathers before them, buying and selling land as they went, in a process of "itinerant accumulation."[29] The less successful were even more likely to sell out, as rising land prices increased the opportunity cost of their low productivity farming.

Summary: labor, financial, and land markets on the frontier

In the 1980s frontier farming does not seem to have covered its opportunity cost in the land market, but these costs were covered in the labor and financial markets. The combination of high returns to capital and labor and low returns to land reduced the advantage to a farmer of remaining long on a specific plot of land, but not the advantage of continuing to farm in the frontier area generally. The opportunity costs to frontier farming apparently contributed to farmer intraregional migration, with high capital gains spurring turnover in old frontiers and financing the opening of new frontiers.

Newcomers: the merchant frontier

There seems to be a two-stage process of frontier occupation in directed settlement projects that is not unlike the traditional frontier process in the rest of Brazil.[30] Original family farmers deforest, leave, and are replaced by newcomers who belong to a higher income bracket and use land for different purposes than did the original settlers.

Tables A.10, A.11, and A.12 suggest that these newcomers, embedded in the 1991 total, were younger and significantly wealthier than survivors in high turnover locations such as Anapu-Pacajá, Alta Floresta–Paranaíta, and São José do Rio Claro. Many were probably not farmers at all, but rather merchants, public servants, and other city dwellers.[31] There is still much work to be done to identify who these newcomers were, where they came from, what their motives were for buying up frontier lands that had already significantly appreciated, and whatever other distinguishing characteristics they may have had.[32] What is clear is that the process that shifts the frontier is accelerating.

Overall performance of small farmer settlements during the 1980s

There are many more causes for high turnover on frontier lands than those discussed thus far (Mahar 1989).[33] Tables A.12 to A.43 describe directed colonization in the Amazon frontier according to the variables defined in appendix B. Time and space limitations prevent a detailed discussion of each table here. Appendix C organizes these variables into a consistent model of frontier farming, and appendix D statistically analyzes their impact on deforestation. This section briefly summarizes the principal findings.[34]

In general, Amazon colonists did well during the 1980s, not only in terms of being able to cover opportunity costs in the labor and financial markets, but also in terms of the absolute values of their net worth (table A.12), which increased significantly from 1981 to 1991.[35] Most (71 percent) expressed the opinion that they had improved their lot in life (*melhorou de vida*) by migrating to the frontier (table A.13), with the highest ratings occurring in low turnover locations (Mutum, Pacal, and Monte Alegre). An even higher proportion (76 percent) planned to stay on their present plot (table A.15), though only 41 percent planned to invest further in these plots (table A.14).

This apparent inconsistency—planning to stay on, but not in agriculture—may indicate that in 1991 these farmers did not expect much from agriculture and planned to diversify into other activities. In fact, as table A.8 indicates, the evolution of agricultural prices during the 1980s was not promising. Except where agriculture was most productive (Mutum), gross agricultural income (table A.16) covered less than half of total household expenditures (table A.17).[36] Many farmers, therefore, diversified into nonagricultural activities, such as wage employment, businesses, rents, transfers, and so on, to the extent that nonagricultural income (table A.18) became generally larger than agricultural income. In Alta Floresta and Paranaíta, agricultural income practically disappeared by 1991. This represents a drastic change from the previous decade, when nonagricultural income was, on average, 10 percent of total income. Nonmonetary, or subsistence income, was measured by imputing market prices to all goods and services produced for purposes of family consumption or production, agricultural or nonagricultural (table A.19). This value also grew as a percentage of gross income (table A.20), from roughly 25 percent in 1981 to roughly 35 percent in 1991 (Ozório de Almeida 1992, chapter 16).

Once current household consumption and productive expenditures were met, current net income levels (table A.21) were lower in Pará (sometimes negative) than in Mato Grosso.[37] Net current income, in this sense, is somewhat meaningless, as it is net not only of productive expenditures, but also of household expenditures. Solvent farmers have positive net current income, and insolvent farmers have negative net current income, which, in turn, indicates whether there is net debt or net investment.[38] High net income figures in Mato Grosso, in the face of declining crop area during the 1980s, indicate that these colonists were no longer mainly farmers, another important change relative to the past.[39] Tables A.22, A.23, and A.24 show, respectively, that one-quarter of the sample had owned land elsewhere before coming to the present location; all had farmed in at least one place before arrival; and the parents of 86 percent of the colonists had been farmers. Yet, as noted in table A.14, less than half of these farmers still intended to invest in their present lots either because the lots were not sustaining family farming (negative net incomes imply indebtedness) or because the farmers were already thinking of moving on.

Investment is difficult to analyze, as it refers to dynamic decisions that go beyond current production. Net investment (table A.25) is defined as investment (all expenditures intended to increase net worth, after the current agricultural year) minus disinvestments (sale of all durables, reduction in stocks of physical and financial assets, and so on).[40] Thus measured, investment turns out to be negative or small in most of Pará but quite large in Mato Grosso. (This result is consistent with Pará's negative and Mato Grosso's positive net incomes.) These differences in investment help explain the pattern of deforestation that was occurring in each location.

The major investment cost item in the Amazon frontier was deforestation (table A.26). Since arrival on the lot, by 1991 deforestation had eaten up 54 percent of total land held (table A.27). In the public projects of Pará, southerners had deforested a smaller proportion of total land (46 percent) than others (63 percent), but this is because, more than the decade, southerners were purchasing new forested plots and expanding their holdings more rapidly than others, especially in Anapu-Pacajá. In Monte Alegre, the oldest colonization project, plots were already over 80 percent deforested. Among the private projects of Mato Grosso, the largest plots and the greatest deforesters were, by far, the colonists of Mutum, who had already cleared 69 percent of their lands by 1991. The pace of deforestation varied widely from place to place in 1991 alone (table A.28). Overall, it appeared to be approximately 8.9 percent per year: 3 percent in Pará and 18 percent in Mato Grosso. But most of Mato Grosso's projects were deforested at around only 1.5 percent a year, while Mutum, with the largest plots, was going at 29 percent. In sum, colonists with lower net agricultural incomes (as was generally the case in Pará) had less left over for investment and deforested less; colonists with higher net agricultural incomes (as was the case in Pacajá, the exception in Pará, and in Mutum in Mato Grosso) had more left over for investment and deforested more. The source of income apparently matters, as farmers with relatively high nonagricultural income (as was the case in Alta Floresta) deforested less, despite the fact that they did have positive balances left over for investment.[41]

Interestingly enough, fully 83 percent of Mutum colonists, who deforested the most, declared that forest preservation is important (table A.30). Yet only 4 percent of them perceived that loss of soil fertility might become a problem (table A.31), contrary to the rest of the sample (43 percent), and none of them practiced any kind of conservation technique, such as crop or area rotation, compared to 21 percent overall (table A.32). Those who were least worried about soil fertility and conservation were located in projects with the highest farmer turnover: Anapu-Pacajá in Pará and Alta Floresta–Paranaíta in Mato Grosso. Thus, low soil fertility to begin with, rather than eventual loss of soil fertility, may have had an important association with the exodus from these locations.[42]

Market conditions may also have had an important influence on colonists' performance (Repetto 1989). Insufficient storage facilities generally led farmers to sell 82 percent of their product during the first three months after harvest (table A.33). Distance to market (table A.34) and insufficient transport facilities led them to sell 53 percent at the farm gate (table A.35). Mutum and Monte Alegre, however, due to active cooperatives, sold only around

10 percent at the farm gate. For the same reason, agricultural credit was also greatest for Monte Alegre and especially for Mutum (table A.36).

Loans add to current resources if incoming flows are greater than debt repayment on former loans. If repayment burdens are greater, then current account resources must be used to service debt outstanding. Chronic indebtedness leads to dependence on local merchants and to various debt-peonage conditions that frequently lead farmers to sell out and creditors to move in (Ozório de Almeida 1991b). This important motive for turnover is the hardest to observe empirically, as farmers are loath to reveal their debts or their creditors. For this reason observed indebtedness is deceivingly small (table A.37). Negative net current incomes are a better indicator of indebtedness, as they indicate that farmers are covering their current expenditures either through borrowing from themselves (that is, by selling durable goods, such as cattle) or through borrowing from others. In either case the farmer is insolvent.[43]

The capacity to escape informal sector (usury-mercantile) indebtedness depends mainly on titled property ownership of the land (table A.38).[44] One hundred percent of the colonists in Mutum held such title, as did 84 percent in the whole sample, certainly a much higher percentage than is typical of Amazonian small farmers.

Although many farmers had low absolute income levels, they still earned more than did half the labor force in Brazil. Their net worth, rates of accumulation, access to credit, productivities, and other economic characteristics set them off as part of a small farmer elite within the Amazon. To the extent that such benefits are attributable to the fact that they were in directed colonization projects, then colonization may deserve reevaluation for its social and distributive impact.[45] Yet the environmental destructiveness of colonization is considerable. It contributes to deforestation directly, in the projects themselves, and indirectly, by allowing for high turnover on plots. Turnover fuels intraregional outmigration, which, in turn, promotes further deforestation.

Farmers' Economic Decisionmaking in the 1990s

Given the conditions described throughout this chapter, small farmers in the frontier must constantly make decisions on whether to sell or to keep their land and whether to hoard or to farm the soil. Much in the literature deals with the farmers' discount rate as an important determinant in their patterns of resource use.[46] This section will examine concrete economic factors upon which farmers base their decisions. It is not the intent here to analyze how expectations arise; rather this section describes how such expectations inform the farmer's decisions to continue or abandon farming his plot.

A frontier farmer in the Amazon faces three choices in a sales decision about his land: he may choose not to sell his farm and instead productively farm it; he may choose not to sell, but leave his plot idle, keeping it only as a store of value—that is, hoard it; or he may choose neither to farm nor to hoard but to sell his land at the going market price. To deal with this variety of choices, the farmer must be able to discount, at the moment of his decision, the expected payoff of his choice. Thus his decision depends on the net present value of agricultural income (NPVA) and the discounted salvage value of land (NPVL)[47] as computed in table A.42.[48] By adding both figures, the farmer can determine the overall net present value of his plot (NPV) and compare it to the going market price of land. If the NPV is higher than the price of land, the farmer is likely to keep the plot; otherwise, he will probably sell it.

Comparing the NPV to the going market price of land, we found that in half the sampled locations farmers would be better off selling the land. Not surprisingly, this occurs only in locations where the NPVL exceeds the NPVA, that is, where returns to agriculture are not keeping up with land prices. Comparing the NPVA to survival rates on plots bears this finding out: survival rates are lower in areas of relatively low NPVA. High turnover on plots is thus positively associated with low returns to farming, as summarized in table A-42.

In Mato Grosso, land sales peaked in Alta Floresta, Paranaíta, and São José do Rio Claro, all of which are areas of agricultural involution, encroaching pastures, rapid urbanization, and rapidly appreciating land prices. In Pará, land sales peaked in the region of Anapu-Pacajá. In that particular location the NPVA and NPVL were approximately the same, US$33 and US$31, respectively. The average price of land in Anapu-Pacajá was US$59 per hectare, making the NPV only slightly higher than the price of land (US$64 compared with US$59, respectively). As land prices continue to appreciate rapidly in this area, farmers are, in fact, selling out.

For those farmers who choose not to sell, that is, those whose NPV exceeds the going price of land, the question is whether to produce. A farmer is likely to produce only if the NPVA exceeds the NPVL, meaning that his discounted income stream from agriculture must support his decision to forgo the potential gains from land sales. In this case, the farmer has motivation to produce; otherwise his plot will remain idle. The results of this section are summarized in the following matrix (refer to appendix table C.1 for a supporting and complementary argument):

Factors that inform a farmer's decision to retain or relinquish his plot

	NPV > P	NPV < P
NPVA > NPVL	Case 1: keep the land in production	Case 2: sell the land
NPVA < NPVL	Case 3: keep the land out of production (hoard)	Case 4: sell the land

These findings confirm that farming in the Amazon is unlikely to be sustainable unless land productivity and, consequently, agricultural income keep up with land prices. In high turnover locations, the NPVA is not sufficiently high to retain farmers in their plots and motivate production. In other words, the price of land is still higher than the expected income stream from agriculture.

For the 1990s, therefore, the rational behavior of many frontier farmers in the Amazon would be to sell the land at the going market price. The implication of this for regional development policies in the Amazon is evident. Policies should aim at keeping the net present value of agricultural income level with that of land prices (see chapter 6 for recommended policy types). If the gap between agricultural incomes and land prices becomes too large due to rising land prices, the NPVL is likely to rise beyond the NPVA, in which case it would pay not to produce at all but to keep land only as a store of value (that is, in areas where NPV > P). This would further fuel the speculation under way in the frontier land market.[49]

Cost to the global economy of reducing deforestation

Standard microeconomic theory dictates that the price of an asset is equal to the present value of the discounted stream of earnings that it can generate. In the case of agricultural land, these earnings are, generally, the stream of net incomes derived from agricultural production and discounted in time. Despite wide variations across frontier locations, monetary agricultural incomes tend to be low in absolute terms. Among small farmers in the Amazon, the average NPVA per hectare is only US$129.60 (appendix table A.42). If the standard theoretical construct were to prevail, then the cost per hectare to the global economy of buying Amazon land to reduce deforestation could be set as low as US$129.60. Such costs, however, reflect only the productive potential of the land and not the capital gains that can be derived from speculation.[50]

Yet the cost to the Brazilian economy as a whole of reducing deforestation is actually much larger than that of net present value of agricultural income, or the NPVA forgone (Young 1994). This is because monetary agricultural income has been declining relative to total income (monetary and nonmonetary, agricultural and nonagricultural)—at least among frontier farmers. Total income and consumption are relatively high among the same farmers, when compared to economic alternatives in the rest of the economy. Furthermore, frontier land prices are inflated beyond the NPVA, so part of income forgone in the sale of land is the capital gain it affords. The farmer, therefore, would not want to sell at a price equivalent only to the NPVA. The Amazonian farmer is not the only one who forgoes income when he stops planting. Frontier farming feeds a large and growing commercial and processing sector inside and outside the Amazon where income would also be forgone if frontier agriculture were to be reduced. For all of these reasons, the cost per hectare to the global economy for containing deforestation in the Amazon is higher than that immediately apparent from direct measurement of the NPVA or even land prices.

Conclusion: Land Markets and Sustainable Frontier Farming

Much of the literature on the shifting frontier emphasizes penury as a cause of high turnover (Mink 1993). Penury is triggered by the following factors:

- ecological-technological problems (nutrient mining) of shifting agriculture;
- social violence in competition for frontier lands;
- exclusion of many small farmers from official land titling and other formal types of property legitimation procedures; and, finally,
- economic push factors, such as indebtedness and debt peonage.

Although relevant, however, penury is not all that drives small farmers deeper into the Amazon forest. In colonization projects originally intended for the poor, many small farmers leave because they can accrue capital gains by selling their lands. Those who buy the land and move in are not poor at all.

Although farmers may cover opportunity costs in the labor and capital markets and consume at a level three or four times that of the minimum wage, this does not mean that the majority of them are well off in any absolute sense. Houses are rustic, health care is dismal, schooling is minimal, and transport and communications are sorely insufficient. Even if they are better off than the majority of the Brazilian labor force at the same skill level, most farmers are still poor and will only settle down in their current plots if it becomes worthwhile to do so, that is, if they cover their opportunity cost in the land market. Given the pressure of inflated real estate markets on the frontier, however, covering such costs becomes possible only if land becomes highly productive. During the 1980s, high productivity frontiers had high survival rates and low turnover on plots. Conversely, low and/or declining productivity frontiers had low survival rates, and turnover was high. Even some colonists with relatively high incomes and net worth withdrew from agriculture and converted their lands into pastures or even sold their plots and moved away. Newcomers were not eager to farm the deforested land but mostly held it for speculative purposes. Frontier land markets fueled high turnover among all but the best farming communities.

In high turnover locations, those who moved in, and those who remained behind, became disenchanted with agriculture. Poor prices, poor marketing, poor credit facilities, and weak institutions led them to diversify into pasturing and nonfarming activities. They showed concern about soil fertility, professed to practice some forms of conservation techniques, planted little, and deforested little (about 2 percent of their holdings per year). In low turnover locations, agriculture boomed, with little worry about conservation or loss of soil fertility. Lots expanded by incorporation of new areas, credit was available, and deforestation proceeded at around 20 percent per year. Thus, on one the hand, high turnover seems to be associated with agricultural involution and nonproductive use of already deforested lands. On the other hand, low turnover seems to be associated with agricultural expansion and rapid deforestation.

In 1991, the price of land in many locations was higher than the overall net present value (NPV) of potential earnings in any given plot, prompting farmers to sell. Where the NPV was higher than land prices, but returns to land (NPVL) were still higher than returns to agricultural production (NPVA), a farmer kept his plot but did not farm it, holding it instead as a store of value. Land sales (which occur when the NPV is lower than the price of land) and speculation (which occurs when the NPV is higher than the price of land, but the NPVA is lower than the NPVL) constitute the heart of high turnover rates in Amazon settlements.

Thus, private benefits of settlements (as indicated by high intensiveness and falling turnover) per unit of environmental cost (as indicated by deforested area) evolved differently throughout the frontier. The outcome appears to have been a general decline in sustainability. In low productivity frontiers, this was due to a decline in private benefits from settlement, as intensiveness decreased and turnover increased. Here, the environmental cost of settlement increased slowly, as deforestation rates were relatively low.

In high productivity frontiers, on the other hand, the rise in environmental costs was the main cause of decreased sustainability. Here, the private benefits of settlement were high, because intensiveness was relatively high and turnover relatively low. Environmental costs rose rapidly as deforestation increased, sometimes at alarming rates.

This chapter analyzed one factor that would increase the sustainability of frontier farming: reducing turnover on plots. Policies that would increase agricultural prices and/or agricultural productivity on the frontier would help farmers resist giving into the pressure of frontier land markets, thus diminishing the rate at which they moved out to deforest new frontiers. The problem is that high productivity farming is not only associated with low farmer turnover but also with high rates of deforestation on current plots. Thus, while improved farming may reduce deforestation farther inland, it accelerates deforestation in the current location.

The shifting frontier may always have been a feature of Brazilian agriculture. But the evidence in this chapter indicates an extraordinarily rapid rate of turnover in some locations, suggesting an acceleration in the general rate of frontier advance in recent times. The massive migration to the Amazon in the 1970s increased the stock of small farmers to relay forward from old frontiers to new. So, despite the decline in interregional migrations over the 1980s, the flow of intraregional migrations may have sped up, increasing the urgency of finding ways to improve farming without accelerating deforestation on already occupied plots.

Notes

1. Directed colonization projects are public (official) or private. While official projects were promoted by the government, private settlement companies developed their own type of project. For a description of the two types, see Ozório de Almeida (1992, chapter 8). This source also contains a description of the directed colonization program in Brazil and detailed information on empirical procedures. For a treatment of spontaneous colonization see Barbira-Scazzocchio (1980), Moran (1982), Musumecci (1988), Porto Tavares (1972), Velho (1981), and Wesche and Bruneau (1990).

2. See Feder and Feeny (1991).

3. A preliminary test for the relationship between tenure security and deforestation is presented in chapter 5 and in Pearce and Warford (1993, chapter 1). Goodland and Daly (1993), Lopez (1992), and Lopez and Niklitschek (1991) explain the linkage among secure tenure, poverty, and environmental degradation.

4. The going minimum wage rate is an overestimate of the opportunity cost to small-farmer labor. It does not take into account the probability of earning less (for example, 50 percent in Brazil overall), which should be discounted. So the comparison made in this chapter is unfavorable to the frontier small farming alternative.

5. In Portuguese, capital market (*mercado de capital*) refers to financial markets in general; in the United States, capital market sometimes refers only to long-term financing. In this text no distinction is made between long- and short-term capital markets. Also, see the formula for the calculation of the accumulation rates in appendix C.1.3, expression 5.

6. The price of land was observed independent of construction and improvements (which were counted as a separate part of net worth) and of use. The price of different types of land—forested lands, cleared lands, lands covered with permanent crops, fallow lands, and lands considered not suitable for agriculture—were valued separately, then the microregional gradient of prices was applied to the proportion of different uses in sampled plots. This method minimizes the tendency for land price to become correlated with productivity variations and preserves the exogenous components of land price with respect to land productivity and behavioral variables. This point is crucial to the analysis of turnover on plots and speculative versus productive deforestation (the subject of chapter 5 and appendix C).

7. Although the rate of return to capital may be high among large firms, it is compressed to a minimum among small firms, which represent the main occupational possibilities for rural-urban migrants. Thus, small farmers do not have access to the high rates reported for Amazon merchants in the previous chapter but can expect the low rates typical of microenterprises, especially those in the informal sector. See Ozório de Almeida and Graham (1994) for a discussion of the rates of return to capital in the informal sector.

8. The benefit of small-farmer settlement for nonfarmers, such as users of roads, and those employed by surveying, zoning, extension, and titling agencies, as well as in physical and legal infrastructure projects, located outside settlement projects, will not be taken into account nor will general increases throughout the economy in opportunity costs of Amazon farming. This means omitting discussion of improvements in employment, incomes, income distribution, small firm earnings, interest rates on savings certificates, and other factors in the economy as a whole that would reduce the demand for frontier settlement. These issues are much broader than that of Amazon settlement itself, involving a discussion of the use of policies to combat recession, promote development, and so on. The policies investigated here are only those that directly benefit small farmers already settled in the Amazon.

One important point will be taken up, however—that of the relationship between the economic crisis in Brazil and deforestation. As the crisis is resolved, the opportunity cost of frontier farming should rise and the rate of deforestation fall. This suggests that the decline in interregional migration to the Amazon during the 1980s was not caused by the economic crisis in and of itself, but by overall structural shifts in the population and economy. This is a significant point because it contradicts dominant expectations in the literature.

9. The issue of valuation of natural resources is discussed from differing points of view by several authors, such as Ahmad, El Serafy, and Lutz (1989), Pearce and Markandya (1989), Pearce and Warford (1993), and Stirling (1993).

10. Important attempts at a rigorous definition of sustainability are in Goodland, Daly, and El Serafy (1992). See also Pezzey (1992) for a general review on different concepts of sustainability, as well as Pearce and Atkinson (1993).

11. This and subsequent sections of this chapter rely heavily on the sampled locations described in box 4.1 and in appendix tables A.1–A.43. Prior to reading this section, one should read box 4.1, which gives the names and main features of each sampled location.

12. Consumption figures, rather than income, are used to in order to avoid the problem of double counting with respect to total factor productivity. A household's total income is derived from the productivity not only of labor, but also of capital and land. To divide total income by labor input is to inflate the returns to labor. Total household income, however, was more than twice the value of goods and services purchased and/or produced for the purpose of consumption by household members. This illustrates the importance of farming (non-household oriented) expenses in farmers' budgets. Variations in income were much wider than variations in consumption; that is, richer farmers spent more and poorer farmers spent less on their units of production but tended toward similar levels of expense on consumption per capita. The decision to produce is thus, apparently, a very different one from the decision to allocate resources to family consumption. In this sense, farmers appear to be truly remunerating household labor, by whatever criteria, not merely distributing total income among them. (We thank the participants at the ESP Labor Market Seminar at the World Bank for discussing the issue of total factor productivity with us.) Note that, to the extent that labor's contribution to total income is not fully accounted for, the estimates of labor remuneration presented in this section are underestimates of the true imputed wage in Amazon frontier farming.

13. Schneider (1993), in reviewing the first draft of this text and comparing it to an FAO/UNDP/MARA 1992 study, comments: "In terms of income, settlements in the

North generated incomes four times Brazil's minimum wage—larger than those in any of the other regions other than the South. The ability of settlers to accumulate household durable goods and productive capital… reflects the incomes shown above, with the northern region again surpassed only by the South. Northern settlers more than tripled their assets (increased by 222 percent)" (page 3).

14. Although the farmers in the sample are poor, they are better off in the frontier than they would be elsewhere.

15. Net worth was calculated by including the value of land and that of all fixtures and constructions on the land as of 1981, as well as equipment, other durables, and financial assets. Calculations were in constant 1991 dollars, as seen in appendix table A.2.

16. See the discussion in chapter 3 on the use of the rate of accumulation rather than the rate of return. Note that the use of the rate of accumulation avoids the problem of double counting that would occur if one were measuring the return to capital. The issue here is not how to distribute total factor productivity among the different factors but merely to ascertain how much net worth has appreciated over time.

17. Productive land appreciation can be factored out from total accumulation rates. This is done by using constant prices to recalculate changes in the value of land over a given time period (for example, 1981–91) in patches that are forestland (or otherwise not useful for agriculture) or devoted to crops (permanent or temporary) or pasture, or are fallow. This result (productive land appreciation) is then subtracted from the total variation in land price over the same period, yielding an estimate of the value of speculative land appreciation. See Ozório de Almeida (1991b) for this methodology.

18. As noted in the previous paragraph, there is some double counting in dealing with land separately from net worth. Land is, on average, half of farmers' asset value, and the rate of accumulation is influenced by the rate of increase in the price of land. This means that land is important for farmers' decisionmaking in complex ways and influences his (idealized) calculations in different ways. In terms of deciding where a farmer should put his savings, land price is a factor in calculating the opportunity cost of capital—that is, the accumulation rate. In terms of deciding whether to farm the land or to speculate with it, land price in and of itself constitutes the opportunity cost of farming.

19. This estimate of the price of land does not take into consideration structures and other fixtures on the land. These components are part of total net worth and are included in the calculation of the rate of accumulation. The price of land used here is a microregional average for each type of land use; it is proportionate to the area each plot devotes to different uses but not to the specific productivity of each plot of land. This reduces the estimated variation in land price in each location but does not alter the value of the mean. The estimated price of land rises with agricultural intensity, increasing as land use is shifted from forest, to temporary crops, or to perennials, and declines as land use shifts to pasture and to fallow. Other work has shown that productive land use accounted for approximately 50 percent of the increase in the price of plots during the 1980s, while increases in the price per land-use-type accounted for the other 50 percent. Variations across locations were great. See Ozório de Almeida (1990 a and b).

20. The reasons for variations over time in the price of frontier land are complex. Rental values become capitalized in the land price, according to a distance-to-market

gradient, in a "Von Thunen Ring" effect, as noted by Schneider (1993). Such gradients are, in turn, altered by the changing locus of economic activity and the evolution of governmental, institutional, and other convenience factors. As urban economies evolve differently, so too do their impacts on land prices in various hinterlands. Speculative demand for land also interferes with land prices, influenced by the evolution of local conditions as well as those of the overall economy, especially inflationary experience and expectations. The objective in this work is not to analyze the evolution in the price of land per se but to observe this evolution directly and to analyze its impact on small farmers' decisions to stay or move on.

21. See Ozório de Almeida (1992) for a description and analysis of these programs during the 1970s and 1980s. Also see Brandão and Rezende (1992) for an interesting model of the effect of credit and inflation on land prices in Brazil.

22. See Ozório de Almeida (1990a and b) for comparisons between real estate appreciation on the frontier and in the rest of the economy. See also chapter 3.

23. Exogenous land prices will be an important feature of the econometric model presented in appendix C and estimated in appendix D.

24. This section does not calculate the specific contribution of individual factors of production to total factor productivity. Total agricultural income (derived not only from the land but also from labor and capital) is entirely attributed to the land, causing an overestimate of the returns to land. When calculating the imputed wage rate, the problem of double counting was avoided by using household consumption rather than income. In the case of the accumulation rate, the problem was avoided by taking into account only changes over time in net worth, not in income flows. In this section, however, the problem of double counting could not be avoided.

This overestimate of the returns to land weights the case in favor of productive, rather than speculative, demand for land. Even so, the speculative demand for land predominated. So the conclusions of this section are strengthened, not weakened, by the imprecision in its methods.

25. See Renkow (1993) for a comparative view on the issue.

26. In support of this, scientific studies have found only recently that most cleared soils in the Amazon do not lose their fertility for agriculture. It has been widely believed that most soils in the Amazon region were of an aluminum-and-iron-rich type called lathyritic. When deforested and exposed to weathering, such soils quickly lose fertility and harden. According to the new scientific evidence, however, only about 30 percent of the region has such soil, and most of that is deep within the rain forest. See Rensberger (1993).

27. According to the 1980–85 agricultural census, average rice yields (kilograms/hectare) in the Amazon and *cerrado* frontier areas were:

	1980	1985
Rice	1,266	1,315
Corn	944	1,183
Coffee	904	1,050

Comparing these yields with those of appendix table A.7 is instructive. In 1981, sample yields were slightly lower than regional yields in the case of rice and corn and much lower in the case of coffee. In 1991, sample averages were higher than regional averages for rice and corn but much lower in the case of coffee. Except for coffee, productivity growth in crops appears to have been higher in the sample than in the regional average.

28. See chapter 3 on frontier markets; also Ozório de Almeida (1992, chapters 15 and 18). These findings imply that improvements in roads, marketing facilities, and whatever else might contribute to improving frontier agricultural prices would also contribute to the sustainability of frontier farming and to reducing turnover. Thus, contrary to general expectations, more infrastructure would contribute to less deforestation, not more.

29. See Ozório de Almeida (1992, chapter 21) for an analysis of the process of itinerant accumulation in the Brazilian frontier.

30. See Ozório de Almeida (1992, chapter 12) for an analysis of the two-staged frontier of Brazil in general and of the Amazon in particular.

31. See chapter 3 for a summary description of these newcomers, mostly merchants and other city dwellers.

32. There is still much research to be done on who left, who stayed, and who came into the Amazon frontier small farming communities analyzed here. Much of the data collected in the 1981 and 1991 surveys have not yet been coded or analyzed. This project's research team at IPEA performed the painstaking work of manually correcting and retrieving data from questionnaires and of returning to the field to make additional corrections to the 1991 sample.

33. This section explores the evidence of the 1981 and 1991 samples only and will not attempt to give a general historical overview of the various colonization efforts in the Amazon. For that purpose, see Bunker (1985), Hemming (1985a and b), Lisansky (1990), Ozório de Almeida (1992), and Smith (1982).

34. All variables mentioned in this section are used in the regression analysis performed in appendix D. Acronyms in parentheses refer to the definition of variables in appendix B, to descriptive tables in appendix A, and to regression tables in appendix C.

35. Net worth is the 1991 U.S. dollar value of all assets: land (percent of the total), constructions, equipment, stocks, other durables, and financial holdings. Note that the variation among locations sampled is extreme, going from less than $10,000 among survivors in Anapu-Pacajá (Pará) to more than $500,000 in Mutum (Mato Grosso). In fact, the accumulation of plots during the 1980s in Mutum was so great that owners can no longer be considered small farmers, although they began as such before they emigrated from Rio Grande do Sul in the late 1970s and early 1980s. This case illustrates the variety of Amazonian experiences and the peril of generalization based on an unrepresentative sample.

36. Since small farmers make consumption and production decisions simultaneously, it is impossible to differentiate between these two microeconomic categories in practice. They are, therefore, lumped together into total household expenditure figures in appendix table A.17.

37. Negative net current income is not a contradiction in terms but a common condition whereby current expenditures (household and productive) are larger than current gross income, occasioning flows from the financial account whether in the form of borrowing or dissaving.

38. See chapter 5 and appendix C for a microeconomic model relating income, expenditures, investment, and other variables to turnover and deforestation.

39. The difference in deforestation between solvent and insolvent farmers is important and is analyzed in chapter 5 and appendix C, especially with respect to the typology set up in appendix table C.1.

40. Maintenance and depreciation costs are counted as part of current expenditures (E). See appendixes B and C (sections C-1.2, C-1.3) for a definition of this variable.

41. Possibly many of those with high non-agricultural incomes who deforested less were recently arrived merchants and other city dwellers who held land not for farming but for speculative purposes. See chapter 3.

42. As was seen in appendix table A.7, there is no evidence of loss of soil fertility during the 1980s, but there is evidence of low fertility in what are also high turnover locations.

43. Chapter 5 and appendixes C and D show the importance of farmer insolvency in explaining turnover and deforestation.

44. The regressions presented in appendix D show the importance of including definitive property title to land in explaining small farmer deforestation in the current year and since arrival.

45. Similar findings by FAO/INCRA, based on a much larger sample of agrarian reform projects all over Brazil, indicate that the cost/benefit ratio for small-farmer settlements may be much more favorable than supposed. See Ozório de Almeida (1992, page 618) for a rough approximation of the cost-benefit ratio (1.5) for directed colonization in the Amazon during the 1970s.

46. See, for example, Schneider (1993) on the *imediatismo* that affects small-farmer behavior in the Brazilian Amazon.

47. The net present value of agricultural income (NPVA) is the value today of the future income stream that can be generated by agricultural production, discounted according to the interest rate. The discounted salvage value of land (NPVL) is the value today of the land price per hectare at some future date, discounted according to the interest rate. Farmers take past experience into account in their expectations regarding the evolution of land prices for the 1990s by applying to the 1991 land prices the same yearly rate of increase that occurred during the 1980s.

48. The NPVA and NPVL were computed for a ten-year period—the 1980s—by discounting current agricultural income and current land prices at the relevant rate. In this case the opportunity cost of capital (the interest rate on savings certificates) was taken to be the appropriate discount rate.

49. This trend is evident in our sample. In the state of Mato Grosso, where most of the land sales are taking place, the NPVL is already greater than the NPVA. Speculation in that area is triggered by the presence of a large class of urban ranchers. See chapter 3 for details.

50. With respect to the cost for the global economy of stopping Amazon deforestation, see Pearce and Warford (1993) and Pearce and Atkinson (1993).

CHAPTER 5

Productive and Speculative Deforestation by Frontier Small Farmers

In any frontier, farmers' deforestation activities may be taken as a form of demand for land. Such demand may be for agricultural purposes, which would imply productive deforestation, or for speculative purposes, which would imply speculative deforestation. This chapter, and appendixes C and D, test whether deforestation in the Amazon's old frontiers is mostly productive or speculative.

The main finding is that *farmers who deforest for the purpose of agricultural production are sensitive to price and income variations.* Therefore, by managing agricultural prices, levying taxes on agricultural income, and imposing penalties on deforestation, governments could induce productive farmers to deforest less and make better use of already deforested land. Economic policy could thus be an important instrument for increasing the sustainability of small farmer settlements. On the other hand, *farmers who deforest in order to hold land as a store of value respond inversely to variations in prices and incomes.* Many of the economic policies intended for agriculturally productive farmers would probably only reinforce speculative farmers' motives for holding land.

During the 1980s in old Amazon frontiers, speculative motives for deforestation grew more powerful than productive ones.[1] Thus, standard income, price, and fiscal policies aimed at agricultural production lost their capacity to discourage deforestation. To reverse, or at least dampen, speculative deforestation, policies that punish land hoarding—such as a tax on capital gains—and promote good agricultural practices must be enforced. If properly administered, these policies can increase the productivity and solvency of good farmers and punish those with speculative tendencies.[2] Increasing the number of good farmers in the Amazon would strengthen farmers' sensitivity to economic policies that reduce turnover and deforestation and raise the sustainability of Amazon small farming in general.[3] This policy implication is controversial. Good farming in an Amazon location, it is argued, may have a demonstration effect and attract migrants from elsewhere. The influx may pressure resources and swamp the sustainability achieved. Chapter 6 argues against such a possibility.

The evolution during the 1980s in deforestation motives can be seen by comparing total deforestation (since arrival on the current plot) to current deforestation (during the most recent year). Total deforestation appears to have been most directly related to characteristics of farmer background. The most significant indicator was the extent of a farmer's itinerancy, that is, how many places he had farmed before. Also important were farmers' place of origin, whether their parents had been farmers, how much they brought with them, and so on. Deforestation in the current year, however, was much more influenced by conditions of the present location, such as access to credit (the greatest cause of current deforestation), local institutions, marketing systems, and so on. Apparently, it takes time for migrants to overcome past experiences and become responsive to current local conditions.

In order to analyze the economic determination of small farmers' deforestation, appendix C specifies, and appendix D tests, an econometric model of how small farmers' deforestation responds to policies that alter income and land prices.

Appendix C proposes that the demand for land may be static, when there are only current income and expenditures, or dynamic, when there is net borrowing and/or net investment. In the dynamic case, the effect of total income and land price on demand for land is complex. The effect of income depends, in its own right, on the relationship between farmers' portfolio management and agricultural productivity.

Among solvent farmers, if productivity keeps up with rising land prices, then demand for deforestation should fall as the price of land rises, according to conventional demand for a factor of production (land).[4] However, if productivity fails to keep up with land prices, then the demand for deforestation may become speculative, increasing with rising land price, according to a portfolio demand for an asset (land). Among insolvent farmers, inverse relationships hold (see appendix C, section C.3.2). If productivity keeps up with rising land prices, demand for deforestation should rise as the price of land rises, as farmers try to pay off debts by increasing agricultural production and demanding more land. If productivity fails to keep up with land prices, then demand for deforestation should fall as the price of land rises. However, this is not because of conventional demand for a productive factor (land), but occurs as farmers give up on agriculture, sell out, and move away.

Appendix D uses econometric methods to test for deforestation as a demand for land, based on the model specified in appendix C and adapted to the sample of Amazon frontier small farmers described in chapter 4. Appendix D introduces several new variables—origin, destination, and individual characteristics of farmers—and specifies a four-stage estimation procedure for hypothesis testing.

Background

A frontier is a place very different from the remainder of the established economy. Since migrants are, literally, starting from scratch, growth of productive capacity, or accumulation, is their objective. To grow, however, farmers must invest, which mostly means carving agricultural land out of one of the most dense and inhospitable forests in the world. Thus, settlers deforest. The issues are how much or how little they must deforest and how to minimize this environmental cost.

As a frontier develops, markets form and consolidate (see the more extensive discussion of this topic in chapter 3). As transport conditions improve, product, input, and capital markets become more competitive. As they become less informal, interlinked, and concentrated, usury-mercantile ties to farmers are broken and the debt peonage typical of frontier farming weakens.[5] Rural and urban economies grow, and labor markets emerge. As open-access conditions end and private property becomes more widespread, the land market becomes more active. Newcomers—merchants, officials, commercial farmers—who operate in the market economy, bid up local land prices, offering substantial capital gains to pioneers. Farmers must then choose whether to remain where they are or to sell their land and decide what to do next. As pioneers sell, part of the benefit of deforestation accrues to newcomers, who take over the land in old frontiers.

Settlement is a discontinuous process with respect to life outside the frontier. The decision to migrate is based on the opportunities perceived and the resources available at that time. The decision to stay depends on the opportunities perceived and the resources that can be generated at that location. Pioneer farmers typically farm on several different plots, moving with the shifting frontier, before arriving at their current location. Their relationship to the land, thus, resembles that toward variable capital rather than fixed capital. As long as they believe that there is still land available to move onto, many will choose to do so.[6] Sustainable settlement implies continuous farming in one place since arrival on the frontier, and this sustainability depends on how agriculture stands up to alternatives in land, labor, and capital markets of the overall economy. If frontier agriculture covers its opportunity costs, farmers will want to continue where they are and will tend to conserve the land they have deforested. If frontier agriculture does not cover its opportunity costs, farmers will transfer their labor and resources elsewhere. They may seek outside employment, they may sell their land and buy land in another part of the frontier, they may remain in the location and utilize the proceeds from their sale to invest in other activities, or they may revert to agricultural involution, perhaps withdrawing from crops and leaving the land fallow or in low productivity pasture.

The most immediate issue is not how well to conserve a farmer's property, but how long a farmer remains on the land. Ultimately, sustainable settlement will depend on migrants' performance as farmers. To the extent that settlers remain on their land, they do not open up or deforest new frontiers. To the extent that such settlers deforest for productive purposes, such deforestation in their current location can be discouraged by policies that reduce their current demand for land. On the other hand, frontier settlers deforest not only for agricultural purposes but also for reasons of tenure insecurity, speculation, and so on. Deforestation fueled by other than productive purposes is less sensitive to policies that alter the opportunity cost of poor farming practices. The effectiveness of such policies, therefore, in curbing deforestation in frontiers that are already occupied, though not yet deforested, depends on the strength of farmers' productive motives compared to other motives for deforestation. Comparing these motives requires that they be modeled and tested against empirical evidence.

The econometric model of small farmers' deforestation, presented in appendixes C and D, takes a large number of variables into account. It includes not only static, conventional prices and costs for current agricultural inputs and outputs, but also opportunity costs for farmers in the product, input, land, labor, and capital markets. Additionally, the model incorporates frontier-specific dynamic conditions, such as accumulation, variety of economic activities, start-up costs, and balance on financial account to show whether net investment or net indebtedness occurred. Finally, the model takes into account how migrants with different economic, cultural, social, and personal experiences, as well as different attitudes and expectations, responded differently to the diverse conditions of the frontier.

Space and time limitations preclude a discussion of several other important issues, such as risk, information, contracts, technology, market interlinking, life cycle, subjective equilibrium, production function specification, and peasant motivations.[7] The role of property rights and tenure security in the Amazon is very important and is the subject of an innovative and growing body of literature. However, it is beyond the scope of this book.[8]

Productive and Speculative Responses to Land Price Variation

In established economies, land price tends to vary with productivity, which becomes capitalized into land rent and real estate value. This is not so in the Amazonian frontier, however, where many other factors affect the formation and evolution of land values.[9]

During the 1970s, the difference between land prices for lots with similar soils but in different frontier locations was in the order of 100 to 1;

differences were even greater between locations in the Amazon and those in the established parts of Brazil.

During the 1980s, land prices rose in some places and fell in others, seemingly unrelated to the evolution of productivity, though perhaps related to which crops were dominant in that location and to the evolution of product prices.[10] Real land prices are quite low in the Amazon, with hectares still selling at prices equivalent to thirty bags of rice.[11]

The set of factors that determines land values can be considered exogenous to the decisionmaking of any individual farmer; that is, frontier farmers are price takers with respect to the land market.[12] An individual farmer compares the productive potential with the speculative potential of his lot in deciding whether it should be farmed, hoarded, or sold. His response to land price variations will be productive or speculative depending on the evolution of land productivity and his portfolio management.[13]

Productive and speculative response

The productivity of a farmer's land is an important factor in determining whether he will sell the land when its price rises. When capital gains become greater than the expected discounted income stream from the agricultural use of his land, the farmer will want to sell. The decision thus depends on how real land prices and agricultural productivity (an important influence on the rate of return on investments in land) evolve compared to each other.

In *unproductive frontiers*, agricultural productivity is low or declining relative to real land prices. Reduced deforestation and farming involution conditions, such as decreased cropped area and increased pasture and fallow areas, typify unproductive frontiers. Alta Floresta and Paranaíta in Mato Grosso and Anapu and Pacajá in Pará are examples of such frontiers.

In *productive frontiers*, agricultural productivity is high or rising relative to real land prices, meaning land is held for the future income to be derived from farming it, not for the capital gain from its future sale. Increased deforestation and agricultural intensification, such as increased cropped area, reduced pasture and fallow areas, and low turnover of farmers in plots, generally characterize productive frontiers. Pacal in Pará and Mutum in Mato Grosso are examples of such frontiers.

The other important factor determining whether a farmer's responses are productive or speculative is his *portfolio management*. This is the composition of his investments and disinvestments and his borrowings and repayments, which jointly determine whether his balance on financial account is positive or negative.[14]

Among *insolvent farmers*, net borrowing means that future repayment will reduce their capacity to cover current expenditures in subsequent years. For the poorest family farmers, such borrowing frequently takes the form of crop-lien (when payment is in kind, out of the next harvest) or of debt-peonage.[15] Net disinvestment reduces productive capacity in subsequent years, for example, when cattle is sold to pay for current expenditures.

Among solvent farmers, net repayment reduces current income, but there are still sufficient resources to cover current expenses and reduce debt outstanding. Net investment also reduces current income but adds to productive capacity in subsequent years.[16]

In sum, the following are four cases for productive and speculative responses:

A *productive response* occurs whenever a rise in income augments demand for land and an increase in land price reduces demand for land. A productive response can be expected in two instances:

- high productivity lots/solvent farmers, whose high yields and high investment rates lead to a process of accumulation (case 1 in appendix table C.1)
- low productivity lots/insolvent farmers, whose debts and low yields lock them into a debt–peonage condition (case 4 in appendix table C.1).

A *speculative response* occurs when an increase in income reduces demand for land and an increase in land price increases demand for land. This can happen in two instances:

- high productivity lots/insolvent farmers, whose debts are discouraging them from persisting in agriculture (case 3 in appendix table C.1)
- low productivity lots/solvent farmers, whose low yields are driving them out of agriculture (case 2 in appendix table C.1).

Given frontier conditions where all land is originally forested, a farmer's productive demand for land is necessarily a demand for deforestation. Despite wide variations in deforestation rates in early years, and although managed forestry alternatives are important alternative sources of income, there is no way to cultivate the soil without removing the forest cover[17] (see appendix table A.29). As time passes and a higher proportion of forest is cleared, demand for additional land is increasingly met by purchases of already deforested lands and/or agricultural intensification on such land. Deforestation, then, should fit a model of demand for land better on newer rather than older frontiers. The empirical equations specified in the econometric model of demand for land were thus tested on total deforested area (see appendix D).

Deforestation is the main form of investment performed on a frontier. Clearing land of its original forest cover considerably raises its value, even if nothing else is done to it.[18] Deforestation is dynamic in that it increases agricultural potential; therefore, it may be expected to fit the dynamic version of the econometric model better than the static version. [19]

Deforestation was analyzed according to two different measurements. Deforestation since arrival (F) refers to total deforested area of a given plot;

deforestation in current year (F91) refers to areas deforested during the year 1991. Total deforestation is relatively more sensitive to long-run, early determinants whereas current deforestation is relatively more sensitive to short-term, recent determinants.

Summary of Regression Results—Deforestation: Past and Current Trends

Despite very large variations in Amazon settlement and the many determinants of frontier farmers' deforestation, a simple model of productive demand for land accounted for most of the observed variation in deforestation. The largest, most significant, and most consistent positive influence on deforestation is agricultural income; as long as farmers are productive, a rise in such income stimulates deforestation (see appendix tables D.1 and D.2).

During the 1970s, agriculture was the major activity of colonists, so the overall income effect for deforestation since arrival (F) was positive (see table D.1).[20] During the 1980s, however, more and more frontier farmers began to diversify, moving out of agriculture into pasturing and investing in other activities.[21] Wealthier, higher-income, nonfarming newcomers purchased colonization lots for portfolio management, to add to their net worth, as a hedge against inflation, and as speculative real estate investments in the face of rising frontier land prices. Therefore, in 1991, higher total income was associated with less agriculture.[22] The less productive the land, the greater the movement away from agriculture. The overall income effect, both static and dynamic, for current deforestation (F91) was negative.

This process of agricultural involution provokes a "Giffen" positive price effect. Falling land prices reflect diminishing demand for agricultural land, thus reducing deforestation; rising land prices increase speculative and portfolio demand for land. So the overall effect of the price of land on deforestation, past and present, is positive.

Migrant characteristics, especially a history of itinerancy, had a significant positive effect on deforestation since arrival. Present location characteristics, however, had a more important impact on current deforestation: access to credit and local institutions stimulates agriculture and, therefore, deforestation; poor marketing and poor storage conditions hinder agriculture and inhibit deforestation. This implies that improving local conditions for agriculture for those who have been in the location for a while fosters deforestation. Recent migrants, however, tend to be less sensitive to such conditions and behave more according to what they have experienced in the past.

In general, the regressions capture the dominant trend in the sample, that is, the takeover of lots by nonfarming newcomers. So the estimated income and price effects reflect mainly speculative and portfolio management behavior rather than productive behavior. To the extent that agriculture was

CHAPTER 6

Policy Implications: Institutional Improvement for Sustainable Settlement in the Amazon

The population and economic shifts that occurred in the Amazon during the 1980s brought about a speculative boom in local land markets that drove small farmers out of the frontiers they had deforested in the 1970s and into the frontiers they are deforesting in the 1990s. Amazon deforestation will only be curbed if sound economic policies reward farmers for staying where they are and reverse incentives to move on. This chapter proposes that international organizations, NGOs, and the World Bank could assist federal and local Amazonian governments in creating local long-term economic conditions that would make good farming in the frontier compatible with environmental conservation.

Summary of Results

Small farmers in the Brazilian Amazon have typically farmed along many migratory steps. Many were squatters and tenants who moved from farm to farm, living off lands that were never theirs. Some were landowners who bought, deforested, sold, and profited from successive plots. Relatively high returns to household labor and capital, and relatively low returns to land, have kept small farmers moving, shifting the frontier forward.

In recent years, frontier land prices rose beyond the growth of agricultural productivity mainly because of an inflationary economy in general and a prospering urban frontier economy in particular. Physical and social infrastructure increased, while local public and private sectors grew rapidly. Rising land prices set off different reactions among farmers. Many original colonists reaped capital gains and moved from old to new frontiers within the Amazon, which they proceeded to deforest and quit once again. Others held on to their lands but diversified out of agriculture. The more urban groups held on to land mainly for speculative motives. Finally, some highly successful farmers neither moved out of their lands nor abandoned agriculture. On the contrary, they expanded their holdings and increased their agricultural production. They also deforested their land at an accelerated pace.[1]

Thus, small farmers on the Amazon frontier tend to deforest: more successful farmers continue to deforest where they are; less successful farmers deforest wherever they relocate. Meanwhile, land, originally cleared of forest for farming, is being added to the net worth of a nonfarming and mostly urban local middle class.

Market, institutional, and individual contributions to deforestation

Frontier institutions and market structures have seemed to stimulate deforestation and discourage sustainable farming. Tenure-related institutions have not proven capable of handling titling needs. Marketing and transport facilities have been poor, markets concentrated, and agricultural prices depressed. Availability of credit, although declining, still has made forest clearing less costly, because the value of land rises with such clearing, meaning that collateral subsequently increases. Taxation on deforestation, or on the capital gains derived from land speculation, is practically nonexistent. Therefore, the economic conditions necessary for sustainable settlement are not there. Yet settlers have proven to be sensitive to economic conditions; their response to income and prices accounts for most of the variation in deforestation in directed colonization projects.

Total deforestation (since arrival on plot) depends significantly on where farmers came from, what they originally brought with them, whether their parents were also farmers, whether they were landowners before, and how many migratory stops they have made. Current deforestation (during 1991) depends significantly on the characteristics of farmers' present location. Important factors include the type of project they are in, public or private; how distant they are to markets; and what their marketing and storage conditions are. Individual variations, such as age, family size, time on lot, attitudes, and plans and expectations, seem to matter much less, in terms of total or current deforested area, than origin and destination characteristics. Thus, policies that reduce deforestation on the frontier would do so differently among different migrant groups, according to their prior experience and current local conditions.

Productivity factors and deforestation

In the Amazon during the 1980s, low productivity frontiers witnessed high turnover, though deforestation was relatively low. Only in high productivity frontiers was turnover relatively low, but deforestation was rapid. There are different underlying motives for deforestation that change in different circumstances. In productive frontiers, farmers (both solvent and insolvent) cover their opportunity costs in land, labor, capital, and other markets. Increasing incomes in productive frontiers, then, should increase deforestation; increasing land price should decrease deforestation. In speculative frontiers, farmers (both solvent and insolvent) do not cover such opportunity costs, with inverse policy implications. Increasing income in speculative frontiers would decrease deforestation; increasing land price would increase deforestation.

More generally, there does not seem to be a trade-off between the achievement of national macroeconomic stabilization and accelerated Amazonian deforestation. While a growing economy does help to finance settlement of the frontier, a stable one reduces land speculation and slows down the migration of small farmers from old frontiers to new. Moreover, the higher probability of finding a job in a booming economy increases the opportunity cost of frontier agriculture and offers inducements to small farmers to move to alternative activities. Thus, recovery from economic crisis will not necessarily bring about more deforestation.

A Policy Prescription

The appropriate policy package for increasing the sustainability of small farmers in each Amazon location will vary according to local circumstances. Whatever combination of policy instruments the locality chooses to use, the simultaneous goals must be to promote good farming *and* penalize speculation and deforestation. This is difficult, as it implies an apparent contradiction between means and objective: taxing agricultural income to stimulate sustainable farming. If this can be achieved, however, it will contain intra-Amazonian migrations and deforestation both in new and old frontiers.[2] The following are some of the alternatives available.

First, there is an important role for zoning and for promoting settlement only where the land is sufficiently productive to sustain farming income. However, as zoning cannot by itself control the intraregional forces that promote deforestation, since it is the more productive farmers who deforest most, it should be accompanied by a redesign of regional fiscal policy by federal and state governments.

Second, fiscal policy should tax net worth, capital gains from land sales, and deforestation itself. A tax on net worth would increase the cost of deforestation undertaken merely to legitimize property. A tax on capital gains from land sales would increase the cost of speculating in the land market and improve the farming alternative. A tax on deforestation itself, such as a stumpage tax, for instance, would increase the effective price of land, without adding fuel to overheated land markets.

Third, there is a role for the generation and diffusion of appropriate technology. An ample stock of research findings exists in Amazon research institutions, such as at the Goeldi Institute and INPA, as well as in other tropical agriculture research centers in Brazil and around the world, that shows the competitiveness in the Amazon of innovative agroforestry, using combinations of conventional and sophisticated biotechnological techniques. Rural extension must incorporate such results, some of which are widely practiced elsewhere, are experimental, or are still being researched. Application of existing and developing technologies could greatly increase the productivity of Amazon soils. This policy approach does not exclude the use of *caboclo* (indigenous technologies) as feasible and valid ways to achieve a sustainable frontier.[3] Although such technologies tend to be overly romanticized, their use, singly or in combination with biotechnological and other high-tech alternatives, expands the set of tools available to deal with the large variety of local conditions.

Fourth, there is a role for policies that improve market systems, storage, transport, and roads, thus helping to break typical frontier monopsonies and monopolies and improve farmers' bargaining power in principal markets. Marketing conditions must be improved to help small farmers—rather than merchants and large landowners—to appropriate the benefits from productivity increases.

Fifth, the operation of credit and other institutions must be revised to eliminate strong incentives to deforest.

Sixth, there must be conditionality clauses on federal government transfers.

Seventh, all of the above should be developed as locally enforceable instruments, some at the state and some at municipal levels. Democratization combined with fiscal decentralization has distributed proportionately more revenues than responsibilities. The federal government is simply incapable of dealing with the complex set of policies necessary to ensure environmental conservation throughout the country. Local authorities, on the other hand, are now politically and economically capable of taking on this task. This is especially true in the Amazon, where there is the greatest variety of local circumstances and where centralized environmental policy has not been successful. Local-level governance, however, must confront local elites (that is, the same urban middle class that speculates with land) who have become not only an economic, but also a political, force in the region. This political force is likely to offer resistance to the policies recommended here, unless the interest of small farmers continues to receive support from NGOs, the scientific community, and from multilateral organizations such as the World Bank.[4]

Last, in areas where the above set of policies proves insufficient for retaining small farmers, directed settlement projects could be instituted. Such settlements would be different from those of the past; that is, instead of bringing migrants in, their aim would be to prevent migrants from moving out and deforesting another plot. Unfortunately, proposals for such projects have met strong resistance because of the failure of large-scale colonization projects directed by the federal government in the 1970s. This is unfortunate, since failures of the past offer lessons for the future, the main one for today being to avoid merely setting up the projects with mapping, roads, and titling, without creating the policies that would make them sustainable. The main contribution of a 1990s diluted directed settlement would be the provision of tenure security, or property title, an important influence in curbing both turnover and deforestation (see appendix D).[5]

These eight policies aim to reduce deforestation by promoting good farming frontiers that reward migrants for staying in the lots they have already cleared, weaken their motives for speculative and unproductive deforestation of their current location, and reduce economic incentives to move on to other frontiers deeper into the Amazon.

Certain conditions must be met for such policies to be successful. As discussed earlier, one such condition is that these policies generate sufficient local revenues to pay for their local enforcement as well as for the expenses of direct conservation measures.

The other is that successful locations not be overrun by interregional migrants in a perverse demonstration effect. The evidence in chapters 2 and 3 indicates that this is not likely. If and when the Brazilian economic crisis ever ends, the financial and demographic adjustments that it caused will probably have become irreversible. Thus, it is highly improbable that sustainable frontier farming would trigger another Amazon-bound migration similar to that of the 1970s. The establishment of regional equilibrium, therefore, would not be invalidated by a national equilibrium adjustment.

In addition, there are obstacles to the above policies that must be overcome. Establishing zoning, rural extension, and improvements in marketing and credit systems will be a major undertaking. Long-term political resistance to taxes on capital gains will not disappear merely because such taxation will support conservation. Stumpage taxes have been difficult enough to levy on large-scale logging, let alone on masses of small, medium, and large farmers. The failure of earlier directed settlement projects has generated widespread resistance to their revival in any form. Finally, in the absence of national macroeconomic stability, it is questionable whether local policies could have an impact on Amazonian deforestation.

Although all of these issues are relevant, it is not possible to address them in this chapter. The objective here is merely to make explicit what policies are needed to curb Amazonian deforestation, not to provide a blueprint for their implementation.

Economic-environmental policies for curbing deforestation:
a role for international, national, state, and local authorities

Incentives for Amazonian deforestation in the 1990s are different from those of the 1970s and 1980s. Rather than being federally instituted, they are locally generated. Reversing them has become much more complicated than merely repealing central tax and credit legislation. Environmental-economic policy is now the key to achieving sustainability in Amazonian small farming. What is needed is the political will and the competence to design and enforce the policy instruments necessary to encompass a basin noted for its divergent development.

There is a natural role for the federal government in encouraging, monitoring, and coordinating Amazonian economic policy for reducing deforestation. State and local authorities are subject to local opinion and political pressure favorable to raising revenues from economic activity that includes deforestation. The federal government, on the other hand, is subject to international and national public opinion and political pressure in favor of reducing deforestation. The problem is that federal environmental policy relies heavily on command-and-control instruments, which, due to the ongoing economic crisis, tend to be underfinanced and unevenly enforced.[6] Another problem is that economic policies with indirect environmental impacts are not ordinarily seen to be the responsibility of environmental authorities, but of economic authorities.[7] The levying of a stumpage tax to increase the cost of deforestation, for instance, is not a decision that can be taken by an environmental ministry or secretariat, but rather a financial authority. The environmental-fiscal policy field is still in its infancy in Brazil and its practice incipient.[8]

There is a need to develop an innovative system of institutional cooperation for applying economic-environmental policies. Although international institutions, national and international NGOs, and private enterprises could play an important role toward this end, these agencies have tended to focus only on protecting specific locations.

Although such direct conservation measures are necessary, they are not sufficient. The broad forces that are impelling small farmers out of old and toward new frontiers in the Amazon will eventually put pressure on these forest reserves, no matter how well implemented. The conservation of specific remote areas will be short lived, therefore, unless the large Amazonian rural population attains sustainability in old frontiers. The following two sections outline some of the forest conservation programs supported by the World Bank and NGOs.[9]

Rain forest pilot program

The Pilot Program to Conserve the Brazilian Rain Forest was created to support an integrated set of projects targeted to reduce deforestation in a manner that is consistent with the sustainable development of the area's natural and human resources.[10] The pilot program supports innovative grassroots initiatives aimed at harmonizing environmental objectives with improving the standards of living of the more than 10 million people who inhabit the Brazilian Amazon.[11] The program was launched at the request of the Group of Seven (G-7) countries who, along with the Commission of European Communities and the Netherlands, give it financial support. Total financial and technical assistance pledged to the pilot program is US$280 million, of which US$59 million is committed to the Rain Forest Trust Fund, under the World Bank trusteeship.[12] The pilot program is coordinated by the World Bank, in accordance with the agreements reached by its participants, that is, the donors and Brazil.

The participants of the pilot program attempt to coordinate their activities with the activities of other organizations committed to combating the underlying causes of deforestation in the region.[13] Through direct governmental actions and through measures that encourage other agents—individuals, enterprises, and private organizations—to conserve, the pilot program attempts to promote patterns of behavior that favor sustainable development.

Although the pilot program recognizes that unsustainable small farmer settlement is one of the major causes of deforestation in the region, it has no specific instruments for dealing with this issue. The subproject on national forests, for example, states that the "resolution of land tenure issues" is important but does not detail ways in which the World Bank and other pilot program participants, including the Brazilian government, would address the problem or at least have the incentive to do so.[14]

Not unlike the national forests project, almost all other projects of the pilot program allege concern for the shifting frontier. However, actual implementation of tenure-related policies is considered to be the job of the Brazilian Environmental Institute (IBAMA) and the National Institute for Colonization and Agrarian Reform (INCRA). Both of these organizations have overlapping, uncoordinated, and spotty records in the treatment of land tenure.[15] Since the 1980s economic crisis, furthermore, INCRA's institutional capacity to do justice to the problem has suffered severely.[16]

The areas selected by the Brazilian government for the implementation of several pilot projects avoid the settlement issues, as these places are not near land under dispute or areas where the frontier is advancing.[17] Consequently, the projects are likely to be successful in the short term. The issue is how long it will take until the frontier arrives and how these projects will fend off encroachment when it does.

In addition, the pilot program has also created the Indigenous Reserves Project in an effort to protect the people who depend on the forest for survival.[18] Although such areas are important to the survival of indigenous Amazon populations, their success also depends on whether their lands can be protected from encroachment. The intrusion of small farmers, gold miners, ranchers, and others on Indian and extractive reserves has been a recurring problem, contributing to the overall violence in the region.[19] Thus, demarcating and protecting specific areas—be they indigenous or ecological reserves or areas for ecotourism—are necessary but not sufficient to guarantee long-term protection from deforestation

The World Bank is increasingly recognizing the shortcomings of traditional top-down involvement in development projects and has begun to seek ways in which to involve the community in the projects it finances.[20] Toward this end, the pilot program has set up an international advisory group, composed of a broad range of agents and experts. Strangely, however, economists are absent from this group, and their absence may hamper the pilot program's ability to incorporate economic-environmental policies into its agenda.[21] Local economic programs for environmental conservation, if appropriately designed and enforced with pilot program support, would be a powerful complement. Although the pilot program is still in its infancy, a review of its design is critical in order to ensure its long-term success.

Other natural resource management projects with international funding:
Mato Grosso and Rondônia

For the past several years the World Bank's country assistance strategy for Brazil has increasingly emphasized environmental issues.[22] Despite the serious problems of the earlier Polonoroeste projects, the Bank is much better placed today to assist in a more rational development of the Northwest region because of the gradual strengthening of local institutions, improved technical knowledge, and a growing commitment within Brazil to environmental concerns.[23]

The Rondônia and Mato Grosso projects are based on a broad understanding of frontier dynamics and regional issues. Their objectives—improved frontier farming and environmental protection—are not mutually exclusive; on the contrary, issues such as biodiversity conservation, integrated farming systems, and agroforestry are all given equal weight.

Mindful of the risk of relying solely upon short-term conservation measures, such as the establishment of conservation units and reserves, these projects target the reform of economic and financial incentives or disincentives to migration. Their activities are designed to intensify land use in suitable areas and develop sustainable extractive activities elsewhere.

Unfortunately, however, despite good design and understanding of Amazonian dynamics, which were largely missing from the Polonoroeste operations, the Rondônia and Mato Grosso projects are not accomplishing their goals.[24]

Role of NGOs

Sustainable settlement requires agents who are sufficiently flexible to adapt to a highly heterogeneous ecology and society. Large institutions, such as central government agencies and international organizations, are not well equipped to deal with varied local conditions—conditions leaving a role for local governments, private enterprise, and NGOs.

NGOs are burgeoning in Brazil as elsewhere in the world (Goodland 1992). The World Bank is increasingly consulting with them in different stages of project cycles, not without some controversy. Hundreds of NGOs located in Brazil are involved in conservation, education, and social programs in the Amazon.[25] There are at least eighty-three environmental NGOs operating in Brazil with which the Bank maintains contact. Besides raising vast sums of money for conservation, these NGOs have also had an impact on the alleviation of poverty.[26] In the Amazon, different settlement and tenure schemes are being tested by NGOs in collaboration with local authorities and international organizations, and many of these schemes are quite successful.

Although NGOs can mobilize large sums of money, their main contribution is organizational, not financial (Cernea 1988). These organizations are good at mobilizing people into organized structures of voluntary groups whose goals are the achievement of self-reliance and self-development. NGOs could assist small farmers in implementing the best available technologies for the sustainable use of natural resources.

NGOs in the Amazon are already forming collaborative groups, such as the Amazon Working Group (GTA) established in 1991, to assist programs targeting conservation of the forest, including projects growing out of the pilot program.[27]

Summary and Conclusion

Given the demographic and economic shifts that occurred in the Amazon during the 1980s, increasing local speculative demand for land has become the main cause of Amazonian deforestation today, driving small farmers out of old frontiers and into new ones. Local policies that first promote productive agriculture and then tax agricultural income, punish speculation, and penalize deforestation directly could contain such intra-Amazonian migrations.

Substantial institutional development is needed. Environmental institutions must learn to use economic policy instruments to achieve environmental conservation. Economic institutions must learn to wield fiscal and pricing instruments to fulfill environmental objectives. Local governments must take on executive responsibilities previously reserved for federal governments. International organizations must broaden their objectives beyond establishing protected areas, and they must contribute to improving the design and enforcement capacity of local authorities and help to reverse local preferences for deforesting. What is needed is imaginative conservationist economic policies that generate alternative revenues at the local level.

Amazon deforestation will only be curbed when local economic policies make good farming compatible with environmental conservation. It is increasingly urgent to do so in order to give poor frontier farmers an alternative to invading today's forest reserves.

Notes

1. This is true for small farmers only. Although the end of tax havens and subsidized rural credit during the late 1980s considerably reduced the overall rate of Amazon deforestation, that part of deforestation attributable to small farmers increased. Note the case of Mutum and, to a lesser extent, Pacal in the sets of tables presented in appendix A.

2. This approach is similar to that of other authors who also proposed that Amazon deforestation could be reduced by repealing economic policies embedded in general or regional fiscal and credit incentives that rewarded deforestation. See Mahar (1989) and Binswanger (1994).

3. See Davis (1991) for a discussion on different approaches to production and resource sustainability practiced by indigenous people.

4. Accumulated World Bank experience on the institutional aspects of forest management and settlement in other countries, particularly Indonesia and Thailand, would be of invaluable importance in designing policies for the Brazilian Amazon. See World Bank (1994a and b); World Bank (1993a); and D'Silva and Appenah (1993). See also Feeny (1988), Ascher and Healy (1990), and Jessup and Peluso (1986).

5. See Ozorio de Almeida (1992) and Ozório de Almeida and others (1992) for an evaluation of the performance of directed colonization in the Amazon during the 1970s and the 1980s.

6. See UFRJ/USP (1992) and ongoing programs for zoning, remote sensing, vigilance (Projeto SIVAM), and health, among other things. Various state-level environmental programs also are being set up. Baumol and Oates (1988) also present a standard theoretical treatment on the relative inefficient economic outcomes brought about by such policy approaches.

7. See, for instance, the many alternative/complementary suggestions contained in Schneider (1992, chapter 3, section C, especially pages 92–97).

8. Environmental pressure for the repeal of fiscal and tax incentives for agriculture is a good example of economic environmental policy in action in Brazil. See also Margulis (1992).

9. The following section discusses only two World Bank projects, which were selected on the basis of their relevance to this study in the Amazon region. For a broader discussion of other efforts in the region, such as those that involve the Global

Environment Facility (GEF) and other groups concerned specifically with biodiversity conservation, refer to World Bank (1993c) and World Bank (1994).

10. See World Bank (1993b).

11. This excludes the *cerrado* frontier.

12. See World Bank (1993b).

13. Technical contacts on environmental initiatives are frequent between the World Bank and other multilateral agencies, including the Inter-American Development Bank, UNDP, UNEP, and FAO. The World Bank has framework cofinancing agreements with many of the rain forest pilot program participants, and the procedures for cofinancing are flexible and well understood.

14. An analysis of the whole pilot program is not possible here, as its unique and highly complex structure would require a lengthy explanation of the high degree of coordination involved in its various projects and subprograms.

15. See Ozório de Almeida (1992), especially chapter 8.

16. See Ozório de Almeida and others (1992) especially chapter 5.

17. Three projects, namely "Environmental Monitoring and Surveillance," "Environmental Enforcement and Control," and "Ecological and Economic Zoning," will be tested in three areas, one of which encompasses the portion of the lower Tapajos basin contained within the state of Pará. This is an area in the process of conversion from forest to ranching and agriculture, with widespread goldmining. Activities carried out in these areas will test, subject to a variety of conditions and levels of threat of deforestation, the integrated methodology that will later be expanded to other parts of the Amazonian region.

18. See World Bank (1993b).

19. The killing of Chico Mendes in 1988 gained world infamy as an illustration of the conflict between forest reserves and ranching. More recently, more than forty Yanomami Indians, including children, were massacred, possibly by gold prospectors encroaching on the tribe's traditional territory. This violence occurred only eighteen months after the former president of Brazil bowed to international pressure and staked out a reservation the size of the state of Indiana. In 1992, approximately 600 gold prospectors were expelled from that reservation by federal police and their airstrips destroyed. Prospectors, however, long locked in violent conflict with Indians, soon returned. See Blount (1993).

20. See Binswanger, Deininger, and Feder (1993) and Serageldin (1993).

21. In March 1993, the World Bank announced the initial membership of the International Advisory Group (IAG) of outside experts "selected for their scientific and technical knowledge" in areas addressed by the pilot program. The IAG is supposed to provide technical opinions on and analysis of individual projects, as well as technical reviews of projects before appraisal and annual reviews. The IAG is composed of twelve members, of whom four are geographers, two anthropologists, two ecologists, one sociologist, one forester, one biologist, and one businessman.

22. Unless otherwise noted, data for this entire section were extracted from internal World Bank staff appraisal reports.

23. POLONOROESTE was a program launched in 1980 and supported by five World Bank loans. It was aimed at resolving problems that had been ongoing since the 1970s. Still under debate is whether the environmental costs of the POLONOROESTE projects outweighed the benefits.

24. Even with World Bank involvement (personal interviews with Bank staff in 1993).

25. See World Bank (1993b).

26. Goodland and Daly (1993) cite examples in which the annual budget of certain NGOs exceeded the budget of UNEP because of tax-deductible contributions. Furthermore, they state that "it is ironic that NGOs are free of the problems besetting governmental organizations. The reality is that the latter are not directly accountable, and that they pursue short-term self-interest (for example, tied-aid) to a certain extent" (page 19).

27. The GTA has been actively involved in the preparation of the pilot program's demonstration project, which is a small-grants project designed to fund local community efforts in conservation and sustainable development.

APPENDIX A

Descriptive Tables

This appendix presents information from surveys taken in 1981 and 1991 in the Amazon frontier locations described in box 4.1. The variables for the tables presented here are described in appendix B. The foot of each table contains the reference to the particular variable in appendix B. The 1981 data have been previously analyzed and published (see Ozorio de Almeida 1994). The 1991 sample was based on the same plots of land sampled in 1981 regardless of whether the same farmers were still on the land. Analysis of the 1991 survey is still under way, as is construction of a panel from the 1981 and 1991 data. Although both data sets contain much the same information, the 1991 survey was enhanced and incorporates variables (mainly institutional ones) that had not been present at the time the first (1981) survey was conducted.[1]

All tables separate migrants into "southern" migrants—those from the South, a more developed part of the country (Rio Grande do Sul, Santa Catarina, Paraná, and São Paulo)—and "other" migrants, from all other parts of the country (mainly northeasterners). For each group, the tables contain 1981 and 1991 conditions. The 1991 tables further distinguish those who were interviewed in both surveys ("survivors") from the 1991 total. The tables also distinguish between public (official) colonization projects—located in the state of Pará and run by INCRA—and private colonization projects, which are located in the state of Mato Grosso and run by different private firms and cooperatives. Within these project categories, the tables indicate the means observed in specific projects or locations.

Statistical tests consider the variances among these means to determine if there are significant differences (at the 10 percent level) in variable means among subgroups of colonists. Differences between public and private projects reflect differences in the types of policy settlement adopted. Differences among locations refer to differences in Amazonian habitat and social environments. Differences between southern and other migrant groups refer to differences in origin. Deviations from the mean within groups indicate individual variations. Differences between "survivors" and other inhabitants reveal migration characteristics.

The structure of the statistical tests is shown at the foot of each table. A difference is significant if it passes the t-test at the 10 percent level. Otherwise, the text in chapter 4 refers to seeming or apparent differences. When statistical tests were not performed, this is indicated at the foot of the table. When differences are statistically insignificant, there is nothing at the foot of the table.

Tables

A.1   Survivors [SURV]
A.2   Imputed Wage [IMPW]
A.3   Wage Rate [W]
A.4   Monthly Accumulation [k or ACCUM]
A.5   Agricultural Productivity [QH]
A.6   Deforested Land for Agriculture [AGH]
A.7   Annual Yields [CROPG]
A.8   Prices for Crops and Land [CROPP and LP]
A.9   Rice Productivity [RICE]
A.10 Time on Plot [TIME]
A.11 Age [AGE]
A.12 Net Worth [K]
A.13 Quality of Life [IMPR]
A.14 Plan to Invest [PLAN]
A.15 Plan to Stay [FIX]
A.16 Agricultural Gross Income [A]
A.17 Total Expenditures [E]
A.18 Net Nonagricultural Income [N]
A.19 Net Subsistence Income [S]
A.20 Gross Income [GY]
A.21 Net Income [Y]
A.22 Former Landowners [FORM]
A.23 Itinerancy [ITIN]
A.24 Farming Background [PARNT]
A.25 Net Investment [I]
A.26 Deforestation Since Arrival [F]
A.27 Total Land [H]
A.28 Deforestation in 1991 [F91]
A.29 Deforestation in First Three Years [F3]
A.30 Forest Preservation [OPINION and FWANT]
A.31 Soil Fertility [FERT]
A.32 Environmental Conservation [AGCON]
A.33 Sales after First Harvest [STOR]
A.34 Distance to Nearest Market [DIST1]
A.35 Sales at Farm Gate [GATE]

A.36   Agricultural Credit [CREDIT]
A.37   Net Debt [D]
A.38   Title [TD]
A.39   Family Workers [WKRS]
A.40   Agricultural Land [CROPL]
A.41   Agricultural Price Index [PINDEX]
A.42   Net Present Values of Agricultural Income and Land [NPVA and NPVL]
A.43   Distribution of Initial Capital [K_0]

Note

1. When the 1981 survey was done, there was no expectation that a follow-up would occur. Data storage was inadequate and retrieval is slow. By the time of the 1991 survey, the 1981 research team had disbanded. The 1991 team had different qualifications, understanding of research objectives and methods, and knowledge of what had been done before. In 1993 this new team lost its financing from IPEA, where all previous research was undertaken. Changed priorities in research demand introducing new topics, removing old ones, and reducing compatibility between the two samples even further. The information presented here is an indication of possibilities for further analysis. No discussion of the specific methodological problems of dealing with panel data is made here.

Table A.1 Distribution of Survivors, 1991 [SURV]*

	Southerners				Others				Total			
	Survivors		Total		Survivors		Total		Survivors		Total	
	No.	%	No.	%	No.	%	No.	%	No.	%	No.	%
Pará:												
Official colonization												
Pacal	39	83	47	100	33	66	50	100	72	74	97	100
Anapu-Pacajá	8	67	12	100	24	44	55	100	32	48	67	100
Monte Alegre	6	100	6	100	29	78	37	100	35	81	43	100
Total	53	82	65	100	86	61	142	100	139	67	207	100
Mato Grosso:												
Private colonization												
Alta Floresta	48	63	76	100					48	63	76	100
Paranaíta	20	56	36	100					20	56	36	100
Mutum	17	68	25	100					17	68	25	100
São José do Rio Claro	10	53	19	100					10	53	19	100
Total	95	61	156	100					95	61	156	100
Total	148	67	221	100	86	61	142	100	234	64	363	100

Note: Percentages are averages.
*See appendix B.2.2(1).

Table A.2 Distribution of Imputed Wage, 1981 and 1991 [IMPW]**
(in minimum wages)

	Southerners		Others		All	
	1981*	*1991*	*1981**	*1991*	*1981**	*1991*
Pará:						
Official colonization						
Pacal		4.01^{ab}		3.22		3.54^b
Anapu-Pacajá		1.82^b		2.74		2.49^b
Monte Alegre		1.98^b		1.09		1.19^b
Average	1.1	3.22	0.9	2.55	1.0	2.76
Mato Grosso:						
Private colonization						
Alta Floresta		1.69^b				1.69^b
Paranaíta		1.28^b				1.28^b
Mutum		19.54^a				19.54^a
São José do Rio Claro		1.12^b				1.12^b
Average	1.1	3.83				3.83
Total	1.1	3.66	.9	2.35	1.1	3.23

Note: 1981 differences were not tested.

Lowercase letters: The presence of a common letter superscript indicates that there is *no* difference at the 10 percent level of significance in the following cases:

Vertically (within column)—lowercase letters;

a, b—Between locations (for example, Pacal compared with Mutum compared with Monte Alegre).

*See appendix B.2.3(1).

Table A.3 Average Annual Wage for Family Worker, 1981 and 1991 [W]*
(thousands of U.S. dollars)

	Southerners		Others		All	
	1981	*1991*	*1981*	*1991*	*1981*	*1991*
Pará:						
Official colonization						
Pacal		3.5^b		9.5		7.0^{ab}
Anapu-Pacajá		1.6^b		2.4		2.2^b
Monte Alegre		1.7^b		1.0		1.0^b
Average	1.8	2.8	1.4	4.9	1.7	4.3
Mato Grosso:						
Private colonization						
Alta Floresta		1.5^b				1.5^b
Paranaíta		1.3^b				1.3^b
Mutum		19.0^a				19.0^a
São José do Rio Claro		1.0^b				1.0^b
Average	4.1	3.5				3.5
Total	1.8	3.3	1.4	5.0	1.7	3.9

Note: 1981 differences were not tested.

Lowercase letters: The presence of a common letter superscript indicates that there is *no* difference at the 10 percent level of significance in the following cases:

Vertically (within column)—lowercase letters.

a, b—Between locations (for example, Pacal compared with Mutum compared with Monte Alegre).

*See appendix B.2.3(1).

Table A.4 Distribution of Monthly Accumulation, 1981 and 1991 [k or ACCUM]*
(percent)

	Southerners		Others		All	
	1981	*1991*	*1981*	*1991*	*1981*	*1991*
Pará:						
Official colonization						
Pacal		2.7		2.1		2.4
Anapu-Pacajá		1.2		2.7		2.4
Monte Alegre		1.5		2.0		1.9
Average	2.1	2.3	2.0	2.3	2.0	2.3
Mato Grosso:						
Private colonization						
Alta Floresta		2.5				2.5
Paranaíta		1.6				1.5
Mutum		2.8				2.8
São José do Rio Claro		2.0				2.0
Average	1.8	2.3				2.3
Total	1.7	2.3			2.0	2.3

Note: 1981 differences not tested. No differences found at the 10 percent level.
*See appendix B.2.3(1).

Table A.5 Distribution of Total Agricultural Productivity, 1991 [QH]*

(thousands of kilograms per hectare)

	Southerners	Others	All
Pará:			
Official colonization			
Pacal	62.4	16.0	36.7
Anapu-Pacajá	0.6	0.6	0.6
Monte Alegre	0.9	18.0	15.4
Average	45.2	10.6	22.1
Mato Grosso:			
Private colonization			
Alta Floresta	0.3		0.3
Paranaíta	1.5		1.5
Mutum	1.8		1.8
São José do Rio Claro	0.2		0.2
Average	0.8		0.8
Total	16.6	10.6	14.1

Note: This table reflects productivity per hectare regardless of product. Values reflect output for various crops. For example, Pacal averages are larger than other averages because of widespread sugarcane production.

*See appendix B.2.3(4).

Table A.6 Deforested Land Used for Agriculture, 1991 [AGH]*
(percentage)

	Southerners	*Others*	*All*
Pará:			
Official colonization			
Pacal	41.2^b	38.4^a	39.8^b
Anapu-Pacajá	29.5^{bc}	21.8^b	23.2^{bc}
Monte Alegre	11.2^c	19.6^b	18.4^c
Average	36.0^C	26.9^C	29.8^x
Mato Grosso:			
Private colonization			
Alta Floresta	26.7^{bc}		26.7^{bc}
Paranaíta	24.7^{bc}		24.7^{bc}
Mutum	84.7^a		84.7^a
São José do Rio Claro	33.1^{bc}		33.1^{bc}
Average	36.2		36.2^y
Total	36.1^C	26.9^C	32.5

Uppercase C: The presence of a common letter superscript indicates that there *is* a difference at the 10 percent level of significance between origin groups (Southerners compared with Others).

Lowercase letters: The presence of a common letter superscript indicates that there is *no* difference at the 10 percent level of significance in the following cases:

Vertically (within column)—lowercase letters.

a, b—Between locations (for example, Pacal compared with Mutum compared with Monte Alegre).

x,y—Between states (Pará compared with Mato Grosso).

*See appendix B.2.3(1).

Table A.7 Distribution of Annual Yields, 1981 and 1991 [CROPG]*

(kilograms per hectare)

	Rice		Corn		Coffee	
	1981	*1991*	*1981*	*1991*	*1981*	*1991*
Pará:						
Official colonization						
Pacal	1,097	1,765	859	1,500	200	2975
Anapu-Pacajá	1,068	1,007	704	902	415	658
Monte Alegre	1,010	1,369	941	1,500		
Average	1,077	1,402	844	1,301	307	1,816
Mato Grosso:						
Private colonization						
Alta Floresta	1,541	1,390	1,527	1,573	696	933
Paranaíta**		1,683				
Mutum	1,244	1,861	1,230	2,400	485	
São José do Rio Claro	807		1,092	1,500	599	549
Average	1,352	1,671	1,255	1,824	550	741
Total	1,166	1,502	1,005	1,563	396	1,278

*See appendix B.2.3(1).

**Paranaíta means are included in Alta Floresta means.

Table A.8 Prices for Crops and Land, 1981 and 1991 [CROPP and LP]*
(U.S. dollars per kilogram)

	Rice		Corn		Coffee		Land (U.S. dollars per hectare)	
	1981	*1991*	*1981*	*1991*	*1981*	*1991*	*1981*	*1991*
Pará:								
Official colonization								
Pacal	0.14	0.14	0.09	0.14	0.16	0.17	130	248
Anapu-Pacajá	0.13	0.12	0.09	0.14	0.90	0.17	20	59
Monte Alegre	0.14		0.10				70	87
Average	0.13	0.12	0.09	0.14	1.13	0.17	80	131
Mato Grosso:								
Private colonization								
Alta Floresta	0.13	0.10	0.10	0.09	0.38	0.29	460	258
Paranaíta**		0.14						
Mutum	0.14	0.11	0.13	0.08			220	398
São José do Rio Claro	0.11	0.15	0.09	0.11	0.39		200	267
Average	0.13	0.11	0.10	0.09	0.38	0.29	290	308
Total	0.16	0.12	0.10	0.12	0.76	0.23	190	219

*See appendix B.2.3(2).
**With one exception, all Paranaíta means are included in Alta Floresta means.

Table A.9 Rice Productivity, 1991 [RICE]*

(kilograms per hectare)

	Southerners	Others	All 1981 total	All 1991 total
Pará:				
Official colonization				
Pacal	1,662	2,178	1,097	1,765
Anapu-Pacajá	1,100	990	1,068	1,007
Monte Alegre	3,125	492	1,010	1,369
Average	1,854	1,019	1,077	1,402
Mato Grosso:				
Private colonization				
Alta Floresta	1,390		1,541	1,390
Paranaíta	1,683		**	1,683
Mutum	1,861		1,244	1,861
São José do Rio Claro			807	
Average	1,671		1,352	1,671
Total	1,751^C	1,019^C	1,166	1,502

Uppercase C: The presence of a common letter superscript indicates that there *is* a difference at the 10 percent level of significance between origin groups (Southerners compared with Others).

*See appendix B.2.3(1).

**This mean is incorporated into the Alta Floresta mean.

Table A.10 Time on Plot, 1981 and 1991 [TIME]*
(years)

	Southerners			Others			Total		
		1991			1991			1991	
	1981 total	Survivors	Total	1981 total	Survivors	Total	1981 total	Survivors	Total
Pará:									
Official colonization									
Pacal	6.1^b	16^{bc}	14^b	6.8^b	17^b	14^b	6.4^{Db}	16^b	14^{Db}
Anapu-Pacajá	3.8^{Dbcd}	14^{bc}	14^{Db}	3.7^c	13^b	8.5^c	3.7^{Dc}	13^b	9.3^{Dc}
Monte Alegre	19^{Da}	29^a	28^{Da}	16^a	33^a	25^a	17^{Da}	32^{Ea}	25^{DEa}
Average	6.6^D	17^B	16^D	7.8^D	21^{BE}	15^{DE}	7.4^D	19^E	15^{DE}
Mato Grosso:									
Private colonization									
Alta Floresta	2.8^{cd}	13^{bc}	10^b				2.8^{Dc}	13^b	10^{Dbc}
Paranaíta	1.5^d	12^{bc}	9.5^b				1.5^{Dc}	12^b	9.5^{Dbc}
Mutum	1.5^d	12^c	10^b				1.5^{Da}	12^b	10^{Dbc}
São José do Rio Claro	4.2^{bc}	16^b	13^b				4.2^{Dbc}	16^b	13^{Dbc}
Average	2.6^D	13	10^D				2.6^D	13^E	10^{DE}
Total	3.7^{AD}	14^{BE}	12^{CDE}	7.8^{AD}	21^{BE}	15^{CDE}	5.3^D	16^E	13^{DE}

Uppercase letters. The presence of a common letter superscript indicates that there *is* a difference at the 10 percent level of significance in the following cases:

Horizontally between subgroups (Southerners, Others, Total):

A—Southerners 1981 compared with Others 1981.

B—Southerners-Survivors compared with Others-Survivors.

C—Southerners 1991 Total compared with Others 1991 Total.

Horizontally within subgroups (Southerners, Others, Total):

D—1981 compared with 1991 Total.

E—Survivors compared with 1991 Total.

Lowercase letters: The presence of a common letter superscript indicates that there is *no* difference at the 10 percent level of significance in the following cases:

Vertically (within column)—lowercase letters.

a, b, c, d—Between locations (for example, Pacal compared with Mutum compared with Monte Alegre).

Survivors: farmers who were interviewed in both 1981 and 1991 on the same plot of land.

* See appendix B.2.3(4).

Table A.11 Age of Head of Household [AGE]*
(years)

	Southerners			Others			Total		
		1991			1991			1991	
	1981 total	Sur- vivors	Total	1981 total	Sur- vivors	Total	1981 total	Sur- vivors	Total
Pará:									
Official colonization									
Pacal	44	50	50	44	55	52	44^a	52^a	51^a
Anapu-Pacajá	43	49	49	46	53	47	45^a	52^a	47^{ab}
Monte Alegre	44	52	52	48	55	52	48^a	54^a	52^a
Average	44^D	50	50^D	46	54	50	45^D	53^x	50^D
Mato Grosso:									
Private colonization									
Alta Floresta	42	50	48				42^{ab}	50^{ab}	48ab
Paranaíta	45	53	47				45^a	53^a	47ab
Mutum	36	41	42				36^b	41^b	42b
São José do Rio Claro	46	53	52				46^a	53^a	52a
Average	42^D	49	47^D				42^D	49^y	47D
Total	43	50^B	48	46^D	54^{BE}	50^{DE}	44^D	51^E	49^{DE}

Uppercase letters: The presence of a common letter superscript indicates that there *is* a difference at the 10 percent level of significance in the following cases:

Horizontally between subgroups (Southerners, Others, Total):

A—Southerners 1981 compared with Others 1981.

B—Southerners-Survivors compared with Others-Survivors.

C—Southerners 1991 Total compared with Others 1991 Total.

Horizontally within subgroups (Southerners, Others, Total):

D—1981 compared with 1991 Total.

E—Survivors compared with 1991 Total.

Lowercase letters: The presence of a common letter superscript indicates that there is *no* difference at the 10 percent level of significance in the following cases:

Vertically (within column)—lowercase letters.

a, b—Between locations (for example, Pacal compared with Mutum compared with Monte Alegre).

Survivors: farmers who were interviewed in both 1981 and 1991 on the same plot of land.

*See appendix B.2.3(4).

Table A.12 Distribution of Total Net Worth (K)*

(thousands of U.S. dollars)

	Southerners			Others			Total		
		1991			1991			1991	
	1981 total	Survivors	Total	1981 total	Survivors	Total	1981 total	Survivors	Total
Pará:									
Official colonization									
Pacal	38.7^{cd}	38.9^{bc}	50.4^b	37.4^a	60.4^a	63.1^a	38.1^{cd}	50.1^{bc}	57.7c
Anapu-Pacajá	13.2^d	9.9^c	79.4^b	15.2^b	17.1^{ab}	29.2^b	15.0^d	15.3^c	36.6^c
Monte Alegre	172.9^{Ah}	168.7^{Bh}	168.7^{Cb}	19.7^{Ah}	11.3^{Bb}	11.6^{Cb}	37.0^{cd}	42.8^{bc}	33.5^c
Average	43.9^x	51.4^x	68.0^x	23.3^D	34.6	37.5^D	29.5	40.7^x	45.8^x
Mato Grosso:									
Private colonization									
Alta Floresta	54.0^{Dcd}	64.1^{bc}	106.3^{Db}				54.0^{Dbc}	64.1^{bc}	106.3^{Dbc}
Paranaíta	39.3^{Dcd}	63.4^{bc}	106.0^{Db}				39.3^{Dcd}	63.4^{bc}	106.0^{Dbc}
Mutum	264.2^{Da}	564.1^a	513.0^{Da}				264.2^{Da}	564.1^a	513.0^{Da}
São José do Rio Claro	80.4^c	124.8^{bc}	141.2^b				80.4^b	124.8^b	141.2^b
Average	78.0^{Dy}	164.5^y	176.5^{Dy}				78.0^D	164.5^y	176.5^{Dy}
Total	68.9^D	127.6	147.2^D	23.3^D	34.6	37.5^D	51.6^D	93.7	101.4^D

Uppercase letters: The presence of a common letter superscript indicates that there *is* a difference at the 10 percent level of significance in the following cases:

Horizontally between subgroups (Southerners, Others, Total):

A—Southerners 1981 compared with Others 1981.

B—Southerners-Survivors compared with Others-Survivors.

C—Southerners 1991 Total compared with Others 1991 Total.

Horizontally within subgroups (Southerners, Others, Total):

D—1981 compared with 1991 Total.

E—Survivors compared with 1991 Total.

Lowercase letters: The presence of a common letter superscript indicates that there is *no* difference at the 10 percent level of significance in the following cases:

Vertically (within column)—lowercase letters.

a, b, c, d—Between locations (for example, Pacal compared to Mutum compared to Monte Alegre).

x, y—Between states (Pará compared to Mato Grosso).

Survivors: farmers who were interviewed in both 1981 and 1991 on the same plot of land.

*See appendix B.2.3(1).

Table A.13   Perceived Improvement in Quality of Life, 1991 [IMPR]*
(percentage)

	Southerners	Others	Total
Pará:			
Official colonization			
Pacal	76^{ab}	65^{b}	70^{ab}
Anapu-Pacajá	67^{ab}	73^{ab}	72^{ab}
Monte Alegre	100^{a}	88^{a}	90^{a}
Average	76	74	75^{x}
Mato Grosso:			
Private colonization			
Alta Floresta	63^{ab}		63^{ab}
Paranaíta	50^{b}		50^{b}
Mutum	91^{ab}		91^{a}
São José do Rio Claro	72^{ab}		72^{ab}
Average	66		66^{y}
Total	69	74	71

Lowercase letters: The presence of a common letter superscript indicates that there is *no* difference at the 10 percent level of significance in the following cases:

Vertically (within column)—lowercase letters.

a, b—Between locations (for example, Pacal compared with Mutum compared with Monte Alegre).

x, y—Between states (Pará compared with Mato Grosso).

*See appendix B.2.3(4).

Table A.14   Planned Investment on Plot, 1991 [PLAN]*

(percentage)

	Southerners	Others	Total
Pará:			
Official colonization			
Pacal	44	35[ab]	39
Anapu-Pacajá	65	56[a]	58
Monte Alegre		30[c]	26
Average	44	42	43
Mato Grosso:			
Private colonization			
Alta Floresta	33		33
Paranaíta	37		37
Mutum	39		39
São José do Rio Claro	55		55
Average	37		37
Total	40	42	41

Lowercase letters: The presence of a common letter superscript indicates that there is *no* difference at the 10 percent level of significance in the following cases:

Vertically (within column)—lowercase letters.

a, b, c—Between locations (for example, Pacal compared with Mutum compared with Monte Alegre).

*See appendix B.2.3(4).

Table A.15 Inhabitants Who Plan to Remain on Current Plot, 1991 [FIX]*
(percentage)

	Southerners	Others	Total
Pará:			
Official colonization			
Pacal	82	70[b]	76[ab]
Anapu-Pacajá	82	82[ab]	82[ab]
Monte Alegre	83	94[a]	93[a]
Average	82[x]	81	81[x]
Mato Grosso:			
Private colonization			
Alta Floresta	65		65[b]
Paranaíta	63		63[b]
Mutum	96		96[a]
São José do Rio Claro	65		65[b]
Average	69[y]		69[y]
Total	73[C]	81[C]	76

Uppercase C: The presence of a common letter superscript indicates that there *is* a difference at the 10 percent level of significance between origin groups (Southerners compared with Others).

Lowercase letters: The presence of a common letter superscript indicates that there is *no* difference at the 10 percent level of significance in the following cases:

Vertically (within column)—lowercase letters.

a, b—Between locations (for example, Pacal compared with Mutum compared with Monte Alegre).

x, y—Between states (Pará compared with Mato Grosso).

*See appendix B.2.3(4).

Table A.16 Agricultural Gross Income [A]*
(thousands of U.S. dollars)

	Southerners	Others	Total
Pará:			
Official colonization			
Pacal	4.3^b	3.2	3.8^b
Anapu-Pacajá	5.3^b	1.0	1.8^b
Monte Alegre	6.3^b	2.1	2.7^b
Average	4.7	2.0	2.9^x
Mato Grosso:			
Private colonization			
Alta Floresta	0.9^b		0.9^b
Paranaíta	0.4^b		0.4^b
Mutum	43.3^a		43.3^a
São José do Rio Claro	6.2^b		6.2^b
Average	8.1		8.1^y
Total	7.1^C	2.0^C	5.1

Uppercase C: The presence of a common letter superscript indicates that there *is* a difference at the 10 percent level of significance between origin groups, (Southerners compared with Others).

Lowercase letters: The presence of a common letter superscript indicates that there is *no* difference at the 10 percent level of significance in the following cases:

Vertically (within column)—lowercase letters.

a, b—Between locations (for example, Pacal compared with Mutum compared with Monte Alegre).

x, y—Between states (Pará compared with Mato Grosso).

*See appendix B.2.3(1).

Table A.17 Total Expenditures, 1991 [E]*

(thousands of U.S. dollars)

	Southerners	*Others*	*Total*
Pará:			
Official colonization			
Pacal	14.9^b	3.7	9.5^b
Anapu-Pacajá	2.2^b	2.9	2.8^b
Monte Alegre	14.8^b	17.3	16.9^b
Average	13.0	6.9	8.9
Mato Grosso:			
Private colonization			
Alta Floresta	9.5^b		9.5^b
Paranaíta	9.2^b		9.2^b
Mutum	47.2^a		47.2^a
São José do Rio Claro	8.1^b		8.1^b
Average	15.3		15.3
Average	14.6^C	6.9^C	11.7

Upper Case C: The presence of a common letter superscript indicates that there *is* a difference at the 10 percent level of significance between origin groups (Southerners compared with Others).

Lowercase letters: The presence of a common letter superscript indicates that there is *no* difference at the 10 percent level of significance in the following cases:

Vertically (within column)—lowercase letters.

a, b—Between locations (for example, Pacal compared with Mutum compared with Monte Alegre).

*See Appendix B.2.3(3).

Table A.18 Net Nonagricultural Income, 1991 [N]*
(thousands of U.S. dollars)

	Southerners	*Others*	*Total*
Pará:			
Official colonization			
Pacal	4.1	6.9	5.5
Anapu-Pacajá	-0.3	4.2	3.5
Monte Alegre	11.9	1.5	3.1
Average	4.2	4.4	4.4^x
Mato Grosso:			
Private colonization			
Alta Floresta	13.0		13.0
Paranaíta	34.9		34.9
Mutum	71.8		71.8
São José do Rio Claro	14.9		14.9
Average	27.8		27.8^y
Total	20.9	4.4	14.7

Lowercase letters: The presence of a common letter superscript indicates that there is *no* difference at the 10 percent level of significance in the following cases:

Vertically (within column)—lowercase letters.

x, y—Between states (Pará compared with Mato Grosso).

*See appendix B.2.3(1).

Table A.19 Net Subsistence Income, 1991 [S]*
(thousands of U.S. dollars)

	Southerners	Others	Total
Pará:			
Official colonization			
Pacal	0.4	1.9	1.1
Anapu-Pacajá	0.5	-0.2	-0.05
Monte Alegre	-0.4	-0.3	-0.8
Average	0.05	0.5	0.4
Mato Grosso:			
Private colonization			
Alta Floresta	23.8		23.8
Paranaíta	-2.0		-2.1
Mutum	4.4		4.4
São José do Rio Claro	-1.6		-1.6
Average	11.5		11.5
Total	8.4	0.5	5.5

Note: Statistical tests were performed at the 10 percent level of significance between origin groups, and no difference was found. This is indicative of the large degree of variance this variable possesses.

*See appendix B.2.3(1).

Table A.20 Gross Income, 1991 [GY]*
(thousands of U.S. dollars)

	Southerners	*Others*	*Total*
Pará:			
Official colonization			
Pacal	12.7	17.8	15.2[b]
Anapu-Pacajá	15.0	8.5	9.4[b]
Monte Alegre	31.0	5.7	9.6[b]
Average	14.8[x]	11.0	12.2[x]
Mato Grosso:			
Private colonization			
Alta Floresta	57.5		57.5[ab]
Paranaíta	46.0		46.0[b]
Mutum	156.5		156.5[a]
São José do Rio Claro	29.1		29.1[h]
Average	67.1[y]		67.1[y]
Total	52.1[C]	11.0[C]	36.5

Uppercase C: The presence of a common letter superscript indicates that there *is* a difference at the 10 percent level of significance between origin groups (Southerners compared with Others).

Lowercase letters: The presence of a common letter superscript indicates that there is *no* difference at the 10 percent level of significance in the following cases:

Vertically (within column)—lowercase letters

a, b—Between locations (for example, Pacal compared with Mutum compared with Monte Alegre).

x, y—Between states (Pará compared with Mato Grosso).

*See appendix B.2.3(1)

Table A.21 Net Income, 1991 [Y]*

(thousands of U.S. dollars)

	Southerners	*Others*	*Total*
Pará:			
Official colonization			
Pacal	-6.3	8.5	0.8
Anapu-Pacajá	1.8	2.5	2.5
Monte Alegre	0.2	-13.8	-12.0
Average	-4.6	0.2	-1.4^x
Mato Grosso:			
Private colonization			
Alta Floresta	28.2		28.2
Paranaíta	24.1		24.1
Mutum	72.3		72.3
São José do Rio Claro	11.3		11.3
Average	32.2		32.2^y
Total	22.0	0.2	14.0

Uppercase C: The presence of a common letter superscript indicates that there *is* a difference at the 10 percent level of significance between origin groups (Southerners compared with Others).

Lowercase letters: The presence of a common letter superscript indicates that there is *no* difference at the 10 percent level of significance in the following cases:

Vertically (within column)—lowercase letters.

x, y—Between states (Pará compared with Mato Grosso).

*See appendix B.2.3(4).

Table A.22 Formal Land Owners in the Past, 1991 [FORM]*
(percentage)

	Southerners	*Others*	*Total*
Pará:			
Official colonization			
Pacal	19	21^{ab}	20^{ab}
Anapu-Pacajá	33	35^a	35^a
Monte Alegre	0	8^b	7^b
Average	20	23	22^x
Mato Grosso:			
Private colonization			
Alta Floresta	34		34^{ab}
Paranaíta	31		31^{ab}
Mutum	25		25^{ab}
São José do Rio Claro	22		22^{ab}
Average	30		30^y
Total	27	23	26

Lowercase letters: The presence of a common letter superscript indicates that there is *no* difference at the 10 percent level of significance in the following cases:

Vertically (within column)—lowercase letters.

a, b—Between locations (for example, Pacal compared with Mutum compared with Monte Alegre).

x, y—Between states (Pará compared with Mato Grosso).

*See appendix B.2.3(4).

Table A.23 Itinerancy [ITIN]*
(number of stops prior to arriving at current plot)

	Southerners	Others	Total
Pará:			
Official colonization			
Pacal	1.6^{ab}	0.9	1.3^{bc}
Anapu-Pacajá	2.5^{a}	1.6	1.7^{abc}
Monte Alegre	0.7^{b}	0.9	0.8^{c}
Average	1.7^{Cx}	1.2^{C}	1.4^{x}
Mato Grosso:			
Private colonization			
Alta Floresta	2.3^{a}		2.3^{a}
Paranaíta	2.1^{a}		2.1^{ab}
Mutum	1.6^{ab}		1.6^{abc}
São José do Rio Claro	2.3^{a}		2.3^{a}
Average	2.2^{y}		2.2^{y}
Total	2.0^{C}	1.2	1.7

Uppercase C: The presence of a common letter superscript indicates that there *is* a difference at the 10 percent level of significance between origin groups (Southerners compared with Others).

Lowercase letters: The presence of a common letter superscript indicates that there is *no* difference at the 10 percent level of significance in the following cases:

Vertically (within column)—lowercase letters.

a, b, c—Between locations (for example, Pacal compared with Mutum compared with Monte Alegre).

x, y—Between states (Pará compared with Mato Grosso).

*See appendix B.2.3(4).

Table A.24 Inhabitants Whose Parents were Farmers, 1991 [PARNT]*

(percent)

	Southerners	*Others*	*Total*
Pará:			
Official colonization			
Pacal	91^a	79^b	85
Anapu-Pacajá	83^a	90^{ab}	89
Monte Alegre	17^{Cb}	95^{Ca}	84
Average	83	88	86
Mato Grosso:			
Private colonization			
Alta Floresta	82^a		82
Paranaíta	92^a		92
Mutum	96^a		96
São José do Rio Claro	67^a		67
Average	85		85
Total	84	88	86

Uppercase C: The presence of a common letter superscript indicates that there *is* a difference at the 10 percent level of significance between origin groups (Southerners compared with Others).

Lowercase letters: The presence of a common letter superscript indicates that there is *no* difference at the 10 percent level of significance in the following cases:

Vertically (within column)—lowercase letters.

a, b   Between locations (for example, Pacal compared with Mutum compared with Monte Alegre).

*See appendix B.2.3(4).

Table A.25 Net Investment, 1991 [I]*
(thousands of U.S. dollars)

	Southerners	*Others*	*Total*
Pará:			
Official colonization			
Pacal	-6.2	8.5	0.9
Anapu-Pacajá	2.1	2.5	2.5
Monte Alegre	1.7	-13.8	-11.8
Average	-4.4	0.2	-1.3^x
Mato Grosso:			
Private colonization			
Alta Floresta	28.4		28.4
Paranaíta	24.1		24.2
Mutum	72.8		72.8
São José do Rio Claro	11.3		11.3
Average	32.4		32.4^y
Average	22.2	0.2	14.1

Lowercase letters: The presence of a common letter superscript indicates that there is *no* difference at the 10 percent level of significance in the following cases:
  Vertically (within column)—lowercase letters.
  x, y—Between states (Pará compared with Mato Grosso).
  *See appendix B.2.3(3).

Table A.26 Deforestation Since Farmers' Arrival on the Frontier [F]*
(hectares)

	Southerners	*Others*	*Total*
Pará:			
Official colonization			
Pacal	71.78[b]	74.89	73.30[b]
Anapu-Pacajá	410.25[ab]	164.62	206.19[b]
Monte Alegre	530.75[Ca]	60.70[C]	129.49[b]
Average	177.96	108.09	130.29
Mato Grosso:			
Private colonization			
Alta Floresta	133.18[b]		133.18[b]
Paranaíta	92.89[b]		92.89[b]
Mutum	581.71[a]		581.71[a]
São José do Rio Claro	203.11[ab]		203.11[b]
Average	198.46		198.46
Total	192.24[C]	108.09[C]	159.03

Note: Deforestation occurred not necessarily on current plots.

Uppercase C: The presence of a common letter superscript indicates that there *is* a difference at the 10 percent level of significance between origin groups (Southerners compared with Others).

Lowercase letters: The presence of a common letter superscript indicates that there is *no* difference at the 10 percent level of significance in the following cases:

Vertically (within column)—lowercase letters.

a, b—Between locations (for example, Pacal compared with Mutum compared with Monte Alegre).

*See appendix B.2.3(2).

Table A.27 Total Land, 1991 [H]*
(hectares)

	Southerners	Others	Total
Pará:			
Official colonization			
Pacal	147.61[b]	169.98[ab]	158.54[b]
Anapu-Pacajá	1,194.65[Ca]	240.57[Ca]	402.03[ab]
Monte Alegre	635.33[ab]	67.70[b]	150.77[b]
Average	384.40	171.75	239.31
Mato Grosso:			
Private colonization			
Alta Floresta	274.08[ab]		274.08[b]
Paranaíta	193.35[ab]		193.35[b]
Mutum	845.62[ab]		845.62[a]
São José do Rio Claro	440.01[ab]		440.01[ab]
Average	358.56		358.56
Total	366.40[C]	171.75[C]	289.60

Uppercase C: The presence of a common letter superscript indicates that there *is* a difference at the 10 percent level of significance between origin groups (Southerners compared with Others).

Lowercase letters: The presence of a common letter superscript indicates that there is *no* difference at the 10 percent level of significance in the following cases:

Vertically (within column)—lowercase letters.

a, b—Between locations (for example, Pacal compared with Mutum compared with Monte Alegre).

*See appendix B.2.3(4).

Table A.28 Deforestation in Current Year, 1991 [F91]*
(hectares)

	Southerners	*Others*	*Total*
Pará:			
Official colonization			
Pacal	17.49[b]	1.47	9.75[b]
Anapu-Pacajá	1.11[b]	4.55	3.88[b]
Monte Alegre	8.00[b]	3.03	3.72[b]
Average	14.3[x]	2.92	6.93[x]
Mato Grosso:			
Private colonization			
Alta Floresta	3.95[b]		3.95[b]
Paranaíta	3.46[b]		3.46[b]
Mutum	244.05[a]		244.05[a]
São José do Rio Claro	7.80[b]		7.80[b]
Average	64.15[y]		64.15[y]
Total	43.18[C]	2.92[C]	25.63

Uppercase C: The presence of a common letter superscript indicates that there *is* a difference at the 10 percent level of significance between origin groups (Southerners compared with Others).

Lowercase letters: The presence of a common letter superscript indicates that there is *no* difference at the 10 percent level of significance in the following cases:

Vertically (within column)—lowercase letters.

a, b—Between locations (for example, Pacal compared with Mutum compared with Monte Alegre).

x, y—Between states (Pará compared with Mato Grosso).

*See appendix B.2.3(2).

**Table A.29 Deforestation in First Three Years Since Farmers'
Arrival at the Frontier [F3]***
(hectares)

	Southerners	Others	Total
Pará:			
Official colonization			
Pacal	17.54^b	19.32	18.44^b
Anapu-Pacajá	19.46^b	24.52	23.57^b
Monte Alegre	2.67^b	4.99	4.61^b
Average	16.52	17.99	17.51^x
Mato Grosso:			
Private colonization			
Alta Floresta	11.52^b		11.52^b
Paranaíta	21.27^b		21.27^b
Mutum	135.29^a		135.29^a
São José do Rio Claro	7.02^b		7.02^b
Average	33.56		33.56^y
Total	28.34	17.99	24.39

Note: Deforestation occurred not necessarily on current plots.

Lowercase letters: The presence of a common letter superscript indicates that there is *no* difference at the 10 percent level of significance in the following cases:

Vertically (within column)—lowercase letters.

a, b—Between locations (for example, Pacal compared with Mutum compared with Monte Alegre).

x, y—Between states (Pará compared with Mato Grosso).

*See appendix B.2.3(2).

Table A.30 Inhabitants Who Think Forest Preservation Is a Good Idea [OPINION and FWANT]*
(percent)

	Southerners	Others	Total
Pará:			
Official colonization			
Pacal	66^{ab}	62^{b}	64^{ab}
Anapu-Pacajá	75^{ab}	83^{a}	82^{ab}
Monte Alegre	50^{b}	57^{b}	56^{b}
Average	66^{x}	69	68^{x}
Mato Grosso:			
Private colonization			
Alta Floresta	76^{ab}		76^{ab}
Paranaíta	89^{a}		89^{a}
Mutum	83^{ab}		83^{a}
São José do Rio Claro	89^{a}		89^{a}
Average	82^{y}		82^{y}
Total	77^{C}	69^{C}	74

Uppercase C: The presence of a common letter superscript indicates that there *is* a difference at the 10 percent level of significance between origin groups (Southerners compared with Others).

Lowercase letters: The presence of a common letter superscript indicates that there is *no* difference at the 10 percent level of significance in the following cases:

Vertically (within column)—lowercase letters.

a, b—Between locations (for example, Pacal compared with Mutum compared with Monte Alegre).

x, y—Between states (Pará compared with Mato Grosso).

*See appendix B.2.3(2).

Table A.31 Inhabitants Who Perceive a Loss of Soil Fertility, 1991 [FERT]*
(percentage)

	Southerners	Others	Total
Pará:			
Official colonization			
Pacal	36^{ab}	34	35^b
Anapu-Pacajá	42^{ab}	28	31^{bc}
Monte Alegre	33^{ab}	41	40^{ab}
Average	37^x	34	35^x
Mato Grosso:			
Private colonization			
Alta Floresta	67^a		67^a
Paranaíta	60^a		60^{ab}
Mutum	4^b		4^c
São José do Rio Claro	56^a		56^{ab}
Average	54^y		54^y
Average	49^C	34^C	43

Uppercase C: The presence of a common letter superscript indicates that there *is* a difference at the 10 percent level of significance between origin groups (Southerners compared with Others).

Lowercase letters: The presence of a common letter superscript indicates that there is *no* difference at the 10 percent level of significance in the following cases:

Vertically (within column)—lowercase letters.

a, b, c—Between locations (for example, Pacal compared with Mutum compared with Monte Alegre).

x, y—Between states (Pará compared with Mato Grosso).

*See appendix B.2.3(4).

Table A.32 Inhabitants Who Employ Environmental Conservation Agricultural Techniques, 1991 [AGCON]*

(percentage)

	Southerners	Others	Total
Pará:			
Official colonization			
Pacal	23^{ab}	23	23^{bc}
Anapu-Pacajá	17^b	13	14^{bc}
Monte Alegre	33^{ab}	22	23^{bc}
Average	23	19	20
Mato Grosso:			
Private colonization			
Alta Floresta	16^b		16^{bc}
Paranaíta	25^{ab}		25^b
Mutum	0^b		0^c
São José do Rio Claro	56^a		56^a
Average	20		20
Total	21	19	21

Lowercase letters: The presence of a common letter superscript indicates that there is *no* difference at the 10 percent level of significance in the following cases:

Vertically (within column)—lowercase letters.

a, b, c—Between locations (for example, Pacal compared with Mutum compared with Monte Alegre).

*See appendix B.2.3(4).

Table A.33 Product Sold after First Harvest, 1991 [STOR]*
(percentage)

	Southerners	Others	Total
Pará:			
Official colonization			
Pacal	78	93	86
Anapu-Pacajá	90	77	79
Monte Alegre	61	72	68
Average	78	85	82
Mato Grosso:			
Private colonization			
Alta Floresta	83		83
Paranaíta	78		78
Mutum	77		77
São José do Rio Claro	89		89
Average	81		81
Total	80	85	82

Note: No statistical differences were found at the 10 percent level.
*See appendix B.2.3(4).

Table A.34 Distance to Nearest Market Center, 1991 [DIST1]*
(minutes)

	Southerners	Others	Total
Pará:			
Official colonization			
Pacal	28.3^{ab}	20.7^{b}	24.5^{bc}
Anapu-Pacajá	35.8^{a}	32.8^{a}	33.3^{ab}
Monte Alegre	40.8^{a}	47.6^{b}	46.7^{a}
Average	30.9	32.6	32.0^{x}
Mato Grosso:			
Private colonization			
Alta Floresta	24.3^{ab}		24.3^{bc}
Paranaíta	27.9^{ab}		27.9^{bc}
Mutum	31.0^{ab}		30.9^{abc}
São José do Rio Claro	15.9^{b}		15.9^{c}
Average	25.2		25.2^{y}
Total	26.9^{C}	32.6^{C}	29.2

Uppercase C: The presence of a common letter superscript indicates that there *is* a difference at the 10 percent level of significance between origin groups (Southerners compared with Others).

Lowercase letters: The presence of a common letter superscript indicates that there is *no* difference at the 10 percent level of significance in the following cases:

Vertically (within column)—lowercase letters.

a, b, c—Between locations (for example, Pacal compared with Mutum compared with Monte Alegre).

x, y—Between states (Pará compared with Mato Grosso).

*See appendix B.2.3(4).

Table A.35 Product Sold at Farm Gate, 1991 [GATE]*
(percentage)

	Southerners	Others	Total
Pará:			
Official colonization			
Pacal	77[a]	75[a]	76[a]
Anapu-Pacajá	44[abc]	55[a]	53[a]
Monte Alegre	0[c]	14[b]	11[b]
Average	65[x]	54	58[x]
Mato Grosso:			
Private colonization			
Alta Floresta	60[ab]		60[a]
Paranaíta	67[a]		67[a]
Mutum	9[bc]		9[b]
São José do Rio Claro	56[ab]		56[a]
Average	44[y]		44[y]
Total	53	54	53

Lowercase letters: The presence of a common letter superscript indicates that there is *no* difference at the 10 percent level of significance in the following cases:

Vertically (within column)—lowercase letters.

a, b, c—Between locations (for example, Pacal compared with Mutum compared with Monte Alegre).

x, y—Between states (Pará compared with Mato Grosso).

*See appendix B.2.3(4).

Table A.36 Inhabitants Who Have Received Agricultural Credit, 1991 [CREDIT]*
(percentage)

	Southerners	*Others*	*Total*
Pará:			
Official colonization			
Pacal	4^c	2	3^c
Anapu-Pacajá	0^c	0	0^c
Monte Alegre	33^{Cab}	3^C	7^{bc}
Average	6	1	3^x
Mato Grosso:			
Private colonization			
Alta Floresta	1^c		1^c
Paranaíta	3^c		3^c
Mutum	52^a		52^a
São José do Rio Claro	17^{bc}		17^b
Average	11		11^y
Total	10^C	1^C	7

Uppercase C: The presence of a common letter superscript indicates that there *is* a difference at the 10 percent level of significance between origin groups (Southerners compared with Others).

Lowercase letters: The presence of a common letter superscript indicates that there is *no* difference at the 10 percent level of significance in the following cases:

Vertically (within column)—lowercase letters.

a, b, c—Between locations (for example, Pacal compared with Mutum compared with Monte Alegre).

x, y   Between states (Pará compared with Mato Grosso).

*See appendix B.2.3(4).

Table A.37 Net Debt, 1991 [D]*
(thousands of U.S. dollars)

	Southerners	Others	Total
Pará:			
Official colonization			
Pacal	0.1		0.02
Anapu-Pacajá	0.2		0.03
Monte Alegre	1.3^C	0.02^C	0.2
Average	0.3	0.006	0.08
Mato Grosso:			
Private colonization			
Alta Floresta	0.2		0.2
Paranaíta	0.007		0.007
Mutum	0.5		0.5
São José do Rio Claro			
Average	0.2		0.2
Total	0.2^C	0.006^C	0.1

Uppercase C: The presence of a common letter superscript indicates that there *is* a difference at the 10 percent level of significance between origin groups (Southerners compared with Others).

*See appendix B.2.3(2).

Table A.38 Inhabitants with Title to the Plot, 1991 [TD]*
(percentage)

	Southerners	*Others*	*Total*
Pará:			
Official colonization			
Pacal	87	85	86[b]
Anapu-Pacajá	92	72	75[ab]
Monte Alegre	100	**	**
Average	88	78	82
Mato Grosso:			
Private colonization			
Alta Floresta	82		82[ab]
Paranaíta	86		86[ab]
Mutum	100		100[a]
São José do Rio Claro	94		94[ab]
Average	87		87
Total	87[C]	78[C]	84

Uppercase C: The presence of a common letter superscript indicates that there *is* a difference at the 10 percent level of significance between origin groups (Southerners compared with Others).

Lowercase letters: The presence of a common letter superscript indicates that there is *no* difference at the 10 percent level of significance in the following cases:

Vertically (within column)—lowercase letters.

a, b—Between locations (for example, Pacal compared with Mutum compared with Monte Alegre).

*See appendix B.2.3(4).

**Data not yet available.

Table A.39 Family Workers Older than 13 Years, 1991 [WKRS]*

	Southerners	Others	Total
Pará:			
Official colonization			
Pacal	3.6	3.1^a	3.3
Anapu-Pacajá	3.4	3.0^{ab}	3.2
Monte Alegre	4.5	1.9^b	2.2
Average	3.6^{Cx}	2.8^C	3.0^x
Mato Grosso:			
Private colonization			
Alta Floresta	2.7		2.7
Paranaíta	2.4		2.4
Mutum	2.1		2.1
São José do Rio Claro	1.7		1.7
Average	2.5^y		2.5^y
Total	2.8	2.8	2.8

Uppercase C: The presence of a common letter superscript indicates that there *is* a difference at the 10 percent level of significance between origin groups (Southerners compared with Others).

Lowercase letters: The presence of a common letter superscript indicates that there is *no* difference at the 10 percent level of significance in the following cases:

Vertically (within column)—lowercase letters.

a, b—Between locations (for example, Pacal compared with Mutum compared with Monte Alegre).

x, y—Between states (Pará compared with Mato Grosso).

*See appendix B.2.3(4).

Table A.40 Agricultural Land, 1991 [CROPL]*
(hectares)

	Southerners	Others	Total
Pará:			
Official colonization			
Pacal	25.63^b	31.36^a	28.49^b
Anapu-Pacajá	57.79^{Cb}	10.24^{Cb}	18.88^b
Monte Alegre	33.42^b	6.13^b	10.03^b
Average	32.28^x	16.41	21.52^x
Mato Grosso:			
Private colonization			
Alta Floresta	39.40^b		39.40^b
Paranaíta	6.52^b		6.52^b
Mutum	373.79^a		373.79^a
São José do Rio Claro	53.33^b		53.33^b
Average	86.28^y		86.28^y
Total	70.03^C	16.41^C	49.22

Uppercase C: The presence of a common letter superscript indicates that there *is* a difference at the 10 percent level of significance between origin groups (Southerners compared with Others).

Lowercase letters: The presence of a common letter superscript indicates that there is *no* difference at the 10 percent level of significance in the following cases:

Vertically (within column)—lowercase letters.

a, b—Between locations (for example, Pacal compared with Mutum compared with Monte Alegre).

x, y—Between states (Pará compared with Mato Grosso).

*See appendix B.2.3(2).

Table A.41 Agricultural Price Index, 1991 [PINDEX]
(U.S. dollars per kilogram)

	Southerners	*Others*	*Total*
Pará:			
Official colonization			
Pacal	0.25^{ab}	0.29^a	0.27^b
Anapu-Pacajá	0.17^b	0.26^a	0.24^b
Monte Alegre	0.09^b	0.09^b	0.09^b
Average	0.22	0.23	0.23
Mato Grosso:			
Private colonization			
Alta Floresta	0.23^{ab}		0.23^b
Paranaíta	0.17^b		0.17^b
Mutum	0.08^b		0.08^b
São José do Rio Claro	0.52^a		0.52^a
Average	0.20		0.20
Total	0.21	0.23	0.22

Lowercase letters: The presence of a common letter superscript indicates that there is *no* difference at the 10 percent level of significance in the following cases:

Vertically (within column)—lowercase letters.

a, b—Between locations (for example, Pacal compared with Mutum compared with Monte Alegre).

Table A.42 Net Present Values of Agricultural Income and Land [NPVA and NPVL]

	NPVA[a]	NPVL[a]	NPV (NPVA + NPVL)	Land prices[b]	Survival rates (percent)[c]
Pará:					
Official colonization					
Pacal	176.4	130.6	307.0	248.0	74
Anapu-Pacajá	33.0	31.1	64.1	59.0	48
Monte Alegre	131.7	45.8	177.5	87.0	81
Average	89.2	69.0	158.2	131.0	67
Mato Grosso:					
Private colonization					
Alta Floresta	24.1	135.9	160.0	258.0	63
Paranaíta*					
Mutum	376.8	209.6	586.4	398.0	68
São José do Rio Claro	103.8	140.6	244.4	267.0	53
Average	145.0	162.2	307.2	308.0	61
Total	129.6	115.3	244.2	219.0	64

a. NPVA and NPVL were calculated using data from tables A.8 and A.27. The NPVA calculation [A]/[H] (tables A.16 and A.27) obtains current value of agricultural income given nondeclining land productivity throughout the period under consideration. The NPVA was obtained by dividing that ratio by $(1 + r)t$ for each year over the 1981–91 time span. The discount rate used was 0.06 (the yearly interest rate on the *caderneta de poupança*, farmers' opportunity cost in the financial market). This period was considered because it is approximately the mean time a farmer spends on each lot (see table A.10) and because the study focuses on a decade-long trend.

NPVL calculation: NPVL is the salvage value of the plot at the end of the period under consideration. From table A.8 one obtains (Price 91/Price 81)1/t.100–100 = g, the average geometric growth rate of land prices during the 1980s. Then, NPVL = Price $91.g/(1 + r)t$.

b. Obtained from table A.8.

c. Obtained from table A.1.

*Mean land prices in Paranaíta were included with mean land prices in Alta Floresta.

Table A.43   Distribution of Initial Capital (K_0)*
(thousands of U.S. dollars)

	Southerners			Others			Total		
		1991			1991			1991	
	1981 total	Sur-vivors	Total	1981 total	Sur-vivors	Total	1981 total	Sur-vivors	Total
Pará:									
Official colonization									
Pacal		9.0	16.2		10.4	19.1		9.8	17.7
Anapu-Pacajá		2.7	2.7		8.0	28.9		6.2	24.8
Monte Alegre									
Average	6.4	7.6	13.9	4.3	7.2	17.9	5.0	7.4	16.8
Mato Grosso:									
Private colonization									
Alta Floresta		14.0	23.0						
Paranaíta		18.4	23.2						
Mutum		37.7	73.0						
São José do Rio Claro		42.6	27.7						
Average	28.2	21.7	31.6						
Total	22.5	18.4	28.1				16.5	14.9	24.6

*See appendix B.2.3(4).

APPENDIX B

Empirical Procedures

B.1 Data Collection

The data for this analysis were collected from colonization projects in the Brazilian Amazon in 1981 and 1991. Field work was conducted in Pará and Mato Grosso by staff from IPEA from September to December 1991. Farmers, merchants, and institutions were interviewed to establish a broad picture of the economic, social, political, and institutional conditions of directed colonization in the Amazon.

The 1981 sample covered 498 farmers, 50 merchants, and 100 institutions. The 1991 sample covered 372 farmers, 128 merchants, and 85 institutions. The years 1981 and 1991 were chosen for several reasons. They were near census years, which provide general information on the universe being sampled. They were normal years agriculturally in the Amazon in general and in the sample locations in particular, with no extraordinary positive or negative features. The ten-year comparison, therefore, is not biased, and this is an important issue in a panel with few time-series.[1] Finally, these years covered the 1980s, a period when the economic and political landscape of Brazil changed drastically. This decade is important in evaluating demand for settlement programs during the 1990s.

The locations sampled in 1991 were the same as those in 1981. All were directed colonization projects, some official and some private. Official colonization projects were all INCRA projects in Pará—Anapu, Monte Alegre, Pacajá, and Pacal. Private colonization projects were conducted by different private firms and cooperatives in Mato Grosso—Alta Floresta, Mutum, Paranaíta, and São José do Rio Claro. These locations were chosen based on multiple criteria, including the lack of comparable field studies. Projects in Rondônia were not included in this research because of the large amount of data already collected there.

Locations visited in 1981 were representative of the Amazon frontier. Ten years later, these same plots were no longer frontier areas. By returning to them, the team observed how frontier conditions affect locations in the long run as these areas become incorporated into the broader economy. This methodology allowed for the observation (and quantification) of the economic motives that trigger farm turnover—an unprecedented accomplishment in the economic literature on the deforestation of the Brazilian Amazon.

A random stratified sample was designed in each location, based on population size, access to market, origin of migrants, and time on plot. In 1981, 498 farmers were interviewed, covering 7 percent of the local population in corresponding census districts. In 1991, 356 farmers were visited, all in the same plots of land visited in 1981. The percentage of the universe sampled in 1991 cannot be calculated for lack of complete 1991 census data. It is certain, however, that the percentage is smaller than ten years previously—the sample is smaller and the areas have grown. Many farmers were not reached in 1991 because of farm consolidation and the absence of interviewees in the sample plot. Also, because of financial limitations on the 1991 research, 10 percent of the Trans-Amazon sample was not revisited.[2]

Farmers interviewed in both 1981 and 1991 are called survivors. Those interviewed in 1981 but not in 1991, the old-timers, are compiled with survivors in the 1981 total. Those interviewed in 1991 but not in 1981, the newcomers, are compiled with survivors in the 1991 total. The tables in appendix A present these three totals separately (1981 total, 1991 survivors, and 1991 total), and the differences among them are tested statistically.

Questionnaires measured a large set of microeconomic, agricultural, and other variables of the farming household. All production and consumption activities are considered part of a simultaneous decisionmaking process. When more than one family inhabited a plot of land, a decisionmaker for the entire plot (sometimes a father or a son) was identified. Values for the other households were then added to those of the decisionmaker. Social information (such as origin) was recorded only with respect to the decisionmaker.

Microeconomic variables. The relationship among these variables was established according to standard accounting procedures referring to the most recently completed agricultural year (1980 and 1990). *Current account* refers to net monetary and nonmonetary income measured with respect to agricultural and nonagricultural activities. *Financial account* refers to net monetary and nonmonetary investment and indebtedness—inflows and outflows of financial resources (loans and repayments) and physical investment. *Net worth* refers to the value of all assets at the end of the reference agricultural year (June 30). *Initial capital* refers to net worth brought to the land on arrival. *Time on plot* refers to the number of years spent on the plot. *Imputed wage* refers to the value of all goods and services bought or produced for family consumption, divided by the number of family workers. *Accumulation rate* is the average monthly increase in the value of net worth since arrival. Unit prices and unit costs of main product inputs were also recorded.

Agricultural variables. These variables refer to various indicators of farming performance—productivity, land use, deforestation, and so on.

Other variables. These variables consider the origins, destinations, and individual characteristics of migrant farmers. *Origin characteristics* refer to previous farming location, prior itinerancy, whether parents were farmers, and land ownership. *Destination characteristics* refer to type of colonization project the farmer chose to settle in, land quality, and distance to market. *Individual characteristics* are tenure, age, education, family size, storage facilities, marketing outlet, intentions, and perceptions concerning conservation issues, benefits, fixation, and so on.

Data correction and retrieval are still under way. As information becomes available, more issues will be analyzed than have been possible to address in this publication.

B.2 Data Analysis

B.2.1 Subsamples

1) Total 1981: farmers interviewed in 1981;
2) Total 1991: farmers interviewed in 1991 (but not necessarily in 1981);
3) 1991 Survivors: farmers interviewed in 1981 and who were still on the same plots in 1991.

B.2.2 Statistical procedures

1) Descriptive tables for:
    i) "Total 1981," "Total 1991," and "Survivors 1991;"
    ii) First differences: "Total 1981–91" and "Survivors" means and standard deviations;
    iii) Tests for differences of means by origin of migrants: "Southerners" compared with "Others"; by type of colonization project: "Official" (Pará) compared with Private (Mato Grosso); by location:
        (1) in Pará: Paçal, Anapu, Pacajá, Monte Alegre;
        (2) in Mato Grosso: Alta Floresta, Paranaíta, Mutum, São José do Rio Claro;
        by date of interview: 1981 compared with 1991;
        by duration: "Survivors" compared with "Total 1991."
2) Correlation, regression, and covariance analysis for:
    i) "Total 1981," "Total 1991," and "Survivors 1991;"
    ii) First differences: "Total 1981–91" and "Survivors."

B.2.3 Description of variables

1) Indicators of private benefits:
    Monetary values in 1991 U.S. dollars per year per family:

W wage rate per family worker per year.

IMPW imputed wage (in minimum wages) = (monetary + nonmonetary family consumption)/family workers.

GY gross income = all monetary and nonmonetary incomes.

Y net income = GY − E (see E in (3), next page).

A gross agricultural income = monetary income from all crops.

N net nonagricultural income = monetary income from interest payments + rents + wage employment of family workers + transfers (official and personal) + businesses − nonagricultural monetary expenditures.

S net subsistence income = all income in kind and barter − all expenditures in kind or barter.

K net worth: value of all assets (financial and physical) = stocks of products and inputs + constructions + land + durables + equipment − debt outstanding.

2) Indicators of environmental costs:

AGH deforested land used for agriculture.

F total deforestation since arrival (in hectares).

F3 deforestation during first three years on lot (in hectares).

F91 deforestation in 1991 (in hectares).

FWANT desire to preserve (1 = yes; 0 = no).

CROP intensiveness (in hectares) = land in perennial + temporary crops.

FERT loss of soil fertility since arrival (1 = yes; 0 = no).

CROPP distribution of prices for crops and land (U.S. dollars per kilogram and U.S. dollars per hectare).

3) Indicators of private costs:

E current family farming expenditures = monetary agricultural expenditures + monetary family expenditures. The prices associated with such expenditures are:

p prices of agricultural products.

w wage rate paid out.

h cost of land.

c cost index of inputs.

4) Colonization characteristics:

Destination variables:

STATE type of project in each state (1 = official; 0 = private).

DIST distance to market = time (in minutes) it took to reach plot from local center.

Three different measurements were taken:

DIST 1—distance from plot to nearest market center.

DIST 2—distance from plot to main regional market center.

DIST 3—travel time from local center to plot (in minutes).

QH general agricultural productivity index (kilograms per hectares): quantity (kilograms)/area (hectares) harvested. Temporary crops (rice, soy, corn, manioc, beans, others) + perennials (cocoa, coffee, rubber, pepper, sugarcane, others).

STOR sales during first post-harvest quarter (percentage).

GATE sales at farm gate (percentage).

CREDIT whether farmer receives credit (1 = yes; 2 = no).

INST number of local institutions in which the farmer participates—rural extension, cooperatives, unions, associations, and church.

Origin variables:

ORIG previous farming experience (1 = southern; 0 = other).

FORM former owner of landed property (1 = yes; 0 = no).

ITIN number of migratory stops prior to this location.

PARNT parents were farmers (1 = yes; 0 = no).

Individual variables:

H farm size (hectares)—total area = cleared plus forested land.

WKRS total number of family workers older than 13.

AGE age of head of household.

K$_0$ initial resources on arrival at plot.

AGCON whether farmer practices area or crop rotation (1 = yes; 0 = no).

FERT whether farmer perceives loss of soil fertility now or in the future (1 = yes; 0 = no).

TIME average time on plot (years).

TD whether farmer has title to property (1 = yes; 2 = no).

PLAN whether farmer plans to invest more in agriculture.

FIX whether farmer intends to remain on the plot (1 = yes; 2 = no).

IMPR whether farmer perceives improvement compared with previous condition (1 = yes; 2 = no).

B.3 Exchange Rates

The exchange rates below were used to standardize all monetary values to 1991 U.S. dollars. The exchange rate devalues the Brazilian cruzeiro beyond the average exchange rate to reach what is considered appropriate parity.[3] This correction may be exaggerated and may underestimate 1991 dollar values. This places strict conditions on the analysis of changes over time. Some discussants of this work consider these values and growth rates too high, so analysis should be considered carefully.

June 1991 exchange rate—Cr$346.31/US$.

Monetary correction:[4]

Alta Floresta and Paranaíta: 1991 prices/1.9.

Mutum and São José do Rio Claro: 1991 prices/1.5.

Monte Alegre: 1991 prices/2.39.
All others: 1991 prices/1.
1981 exchange rate (in constant 1991 cruzeiros): Cr$93 = US$1.
Correction factor used: 1.5 x (1981 US$) = 1991 U.S. dollars.

Notes

1. For standard procedures in panel data analysis, see Hsiao (1986) and Maddala (1983).

2. This gap is being bridged by supplementary field work. Data are still being processed and will be the subject of future analysis.

3. According to IPEA.

4. Since locations were surveyed at different times, monetary adjustment is needed to correct for inflation.

APPENDIX C

A Model of Amazonian Deforestation

C.1 The General Model

C.1.1 Current account

Agricultural product is measured over a one-year period, from July 1 to June 30 of the following calendar year. Production occurs according to a conventional production function (Q), which is continuous and twice differentiable in land (H), labor (L), and inputs (C), such that:

[1] $Q = Q (L,C,H) ; Q_i > 0; Q_{ii} < 0;$
for $i = L,C,H.$

In family farming it is difficult to separate the use of fuel, motors, transport, equipment, buildings, and family labor into productive and household purposes. It takes long term live-in observation to separate the use of time and goods into consumption and production functions. Interviews that attempt to differentiate these activities yield inconsistent answers because respondents do not use these microeconomic concepts in considering their activities. The family farming account, therefore, lumps together both household and farming expenditures (E). These include the cost of land (hH), labor (wL), and other current costs (cC).

The *cost of land* held by the farmer comprises purchase, rental, and deforestation costs, weighted and averaged into a unit price per hectare (h). A farmer covers opportunity costs of land if the expected future income from farming is greater than or equal to (h). Given the inflationary Brazilian economy, there is a general tendency for real estate appreciation because land is an important store of value. In a frontier—where population and physical and social infrastructure are increasing rapidly relative to the established regions of the country—real estate tends to appreciate much faster than elsewhere. This raises the rate of return necessary for frontier farming to cover its opportunity cost in the land market.

The *cost of labor* comprises consumption by household workers (self-remuneration) and payments to hired workers, weighted and averaged into a mean wage rate (w). A frontier farmer covers opportunity costs of family labor if (w) is greater than or equal to the average wage in the labor market, at the farmer's skill level. Since half the urban labor force in Brazil earns less than an official minimum wage (MW), the opportunity cost of labor in frontier farming can be measured by this minimum wage discounted by the probability of getting a job at this rate. Recession, unemployment, and underemployment in the 1980s reduced this probability from the level of the 1970s. A decline in the purchasing power of the minimum wage during the 1980s lowered the average real wage in the economy as a whole. Both tendencies have reduced the opportunity cost of frontier farming in the labor market.[1]

The *current cost* of all other inputs, such as depreciation, maintenance, and repairs, is weighted and averaged into a unit cost index (c). These costs are measured in local markets and include transport costs from industrial centers in the south of the country to the frontier. In recent years, roads have deteriorated, energy and fuel subsidies have decreased, and interest rates on credit for the purchase of agricultural inputs have risen. Frontier farming production costs, therefore, have risen compared with those paid by farmers in the rest of the economy. These tendencies have increased the opportunity cost of frontier farming in input markets.

Annual monetary (*current*) expenditures for a family farm are therefore:

[2] $E = wL + cC + hH.$

Agricultural income comes from the sale of a part of the farm product (q) at an average unit price (p), so gross monetary farm income is $A = p \cdot q$. Nonmarketed output (s) is valued at the same market price, so total gross farm income (monetary and nonmonetary) is $p \cdot (q + s) = p \cdot Q$ (GY in appendix table A.20 and in the regressions of appendix D). Net nonmonetary (or subsistence) farm income is $S = p \cdot (s - e)$, where (e) corresponds to nonmonetary expenditures, such as use of farm resources for building (lumber), fuel (firewood), inputs (seed), and so on. Net nonagricultural income (N) comes from hiring out family members, rents, private and official transfers, non-farm businesses, and interest payments on loans extended to others minus interest payments on debts incurred previously ($r \cdot D_{T-1}$). D_{T-1} is debt outstanding and (r) is the going annual interest rate. The sum of net farming income $(A - E)$, net nonagricultural income (N), and net subsistence income (S) comprises total net current income:

[3] $Y = A + N + S - E$
where A, E > 0; N, S $\geq$ 0 or < 0.

Negative net farming income $(A - E < 0)$ can be covered in current account from net nonagricultural income (N) or net subsistence income (S). Interest payment on former debts $(r \cdot D_{T-1})$ reduces the contribution of (N) to covering deficits in current account or to increasing investment resources. Net current income from one year finances farming during the next year, so current income (Y) and its components (A, N, and S) are assumed to be constant over the production period (one agricultural year) for purposes of production decisions and input allocation. The size of this pool of resources determines whether farmers cover current farming costs $(Y = 0)$ or whether they will have surplus $(Y > 0)$ or deficit $(Y < 0)$ in current account.

C.1.2 *Financial account: portfolio management*

Total net income (TY) is given by net current income (Y) plus the balance on financial account (B):

[4] $TY = Y + B$
where $B = D - I$.

Financial account includes two important components. One is net indebtedness (D)—loans received in the current year (D_T) minus principal repayment from previous loans (D_{T-1}). The other is net investment (I), which is gross investment minus depreciation. Net investment has several parts: savings minus dissavings; purchase minus sale of such durables as land, equipment, and cattle; net additions to stocks of products and inputs; construction and manufacture of such durables and *benfeitorias* as fences, wells, and roads; and land-use upgrading, including deforesting, destumping, pasturing, planting temporary crops, and planting permanent crops.

A farmer's portfolio is determined by the combination of investments and disinvestments, borrowings, and repayments that determine whether the financial account balance is positive or negative.

Positive balances in financial account $(B = D - I > 0)$ indicate net borrowing (D > 0), disinvestment (I < 0), or both. Net borrowing means that future repayment will reduce capacity to cover current expenditures in subsequent years. For the poorest family farmers this often takes the form of crop liens (when payment will be in kind, from the next harvest) or debt peonage (when the farmer overworks his family and land to pay off debts).[2] Net disinvestment reduces productive capacity in subsequent years. It is frequently used to cover current expenditures such as selling cattle to cover deficitary current accounts. Positive balances in financial account imply insolvency; in the long run they may prevent accumulation.

Negative balances in financial account ($B = D - I < 0$) indicate net principal repayment ($D < 0$), investment ($I > 0$), or both. Net repayment reduces current income, but it indicates there are sufficient resources to cover current expenses and to reduce debt outstanding. Net investment also reduces current income, but it adds to productive capacity in subsequent years. Negative balances in financial account imply solvency; in the long run they may lead to a process of accumulation.

C.1.3 Investment and accumulation

The decision to invest is not simple and depends on several intertemporal criteria, including the expectation of future income from alternative uses of capital. This decision will not be modeled in this section, as the objective here is not to project current behavior onto the future but to observe the results of past behavior on the present. Past investments determine the net worth of farmers in the current agricultural year and the rate of accumulation they have experienced since arrival on their plots. These variables are indicative of economic performance on the frontier over time.

The *rate of accumulation* is the average annual rate of increase in net worth since arrival (k). Net worth in year (T) is (K_T), equal to the value of total assets minus total debt outstanding. Household and productive assets are lumped together in this total because it is difficult to separate them in family farming. Initial capital—the real net value of all financial and physical assets brought to the frontier by the migrant—is K_0. Given that real interest payments on savings certificates (*caderneta de poupança*) were fixed at 0.5 percent a month in 1991, a frontier farmer was covering the opportunity costs in the use of his capital if his accumulation rate (k) was at least 0.5 percent a month. Thus, current net worth is the result of investments since arrival. Rates of accumulation (k) and net worth (K_T) can be computed as follows:

[5] a) $k = (K_T/K_0)^{1/T} \cdot 100 - 100$
      given $K_0 > 0$.

  b) $K_T = K_0 (1+k)^T + \sum_{t=0}^{T} I_t (1+k)^{T-t}$

The rate of accumulation and current net worth are thus functions of initial capital and time on the plot.[3]

A farmer's portfolio determines whether and how much he can invest and accumulate. Farmers with positive financial balances ($B > 0$) are not capable of investing in agriculture and should have relatively low rates of accumulation (low k). These farmers will be called *insolvent farmers*. Farmers with negative financial balances (B < 0) are investing productively in agriculture and should have relatively high rates of accumulation (high k). These farmers will be called *solvent*.[4]

C.1.4 Maximization

For equilibrium, farmers maximize agricultural output $Q = Q(L,C,H)$ each year, subject to the yearly total net income constraint $(TY = Y + B)$, which leads to first order conditions:

[6]   a) $Q_i - £ \cdot (E_i) = 0$
           where $Q_i = dQ/di$; $E_i = dE/di$; $i = L,C,H$; $£ = $ Lagrangean multiplier.

     b) $Y + B = 0$

The marginal effect of factors (L,C,H) on the total income constraint reduces to their effect on current expenditures $(TY_i = E_i)$. Net current income (Y)—and its components, agricultural income (A), nonagricultural income (N), and subsistence income (S)—are assumed to be predetermined, since they are given from the previous year. Therefore, they are not affected by the use of labor, land, and other inputs during the current agricultural year:

[7] $dY/di = dA/di = dN/di = dS/di = 0$
      where $i = H,L,C$.

According to equation [2] (page 110), farming expenditures in the current year (E) are affected by current use of inputs, according to unit costs $(w, h, and c)$

The balance on financial account, in turn, is affected by variations in input use $(B_i > 0)$, because debt repayment and investment both require increasing use of inputs even if they do not add to net current income.

The model has four equations, five exogenous variables $(£,h,w,c,p)$, and six endogenous variables (L,H,C,Q,D,I). It is, therefore, not exactly defined.

C.2 The Static Model

The model has a static and a dynamic version. For the static version, assume that there is no balance on current account:

[8] $B = I = D = 0$

From equation [5], the rate of accumulation would be zero (k = 0), and net worth in year T would be the same as in the initial year ($K_T = K_0$). Under such steady-state conditions, equations [6a] and [6b] reduce to a system of four equations in four dependent variables (L,C,H,Q) and four independent variables ($£$, w/p, c/p, h/p) with product price (p) as numéraire. Thus:

[9]   a) $Q_i - £ \cdot E_i = 0$

where Q_i = dQ/di is the marginal productivity of factor i = L,C,H; E_i = w/p,c/p,h/p.

b)   Y = 0

In equilibrium, equation [9] is exactly satisfied, and each productive input (L,C,H) is used up to the point where its marginal productivity (Q_i) is equal to its opportunity cost, which is its real market price (w/p, c/p, h/p). If second-order conditions for a maximum are satisfied, these equations jointly determine the demand for labor, inputs, and land as well as the supply of agricultural product. Equation [9a] represents the first-order condition in which marginal productivities are proportional to real input costs. In particular, the marginal productivity of land should be proportional to the real price of land:

[10]   dQ/dH = $£ \cdot$h/p

where $£$ is a positive constant.

Demand equations for agricultural inputs L,C,H are derived from equation [9] as functions of real input costs and net income. In particular, the derived demand for land (H) is:

[11]   H = H (w/p, c/p, h/p, Y).

Given the numerous factors that determine variation in farmer behavior, equation [11] can be considered stochastic and to include, on first approximation, a normally distributed random error term (v). As an initial approach to econometric analysis, the empirical steady-state deforestation equation is:

[12] $H = a_0 + a_1 \cdot h/p + a_2 \cdot w/p + a_3 \cdot c/p + a_4 \cdot Y + v$

where a_0 is the intercept, a_j (j = 1,...,4) are the coefficients, and v is the error term to be estimated. A variant of equation [12] that takes into account different sources of net income is:

[13] $H' = a_0' + a_1' \cdot h/p + a_2' \cdot w/p + a_3' \cdot c/p + a_4' \cdot A + a_5' \cdot N + a_6' \cdot S + v'$

The farmer no longer maximizes output during the current agricultural year, but maximizes over a longer period. In this dynamic system, both indebtedness and investment occur $(D,I \neq 0)$. Demand for current agricultural inputs (L,C,H) is derived from equation [14] as functions of marginal expenditure $(E_i = w/p, h/p, c/p)$, as before, plus marginal balance on financial account $(B_i = D_i - I_i)$. For the purpose of exploratory estimation, one may single out from [14a] an equation for dynamic empirical demand for land:

[15] $H = b_0 + b_1 \cdot h/p + b_2 \cdot w/p + b_3 \cdot c/p + b_4 \cdot TY + u$

where $(TY = Y+B)$ is the total income variable, b_0 is the intercept, b_j $(j = 1,...,4)$ are the coefficients, and u is the error term to be estimated.

An alternative specification for the above equation is to separate total income into its components in current account (Y) and financial account (B), so that

[16] $H' = b_0' + b_1' \cdot h/p + b_2' \cdot w/p + b_3' \cdot c/p + b_4' \cdot Y + b_5' \cdot B + u'$

where b_0' is the intercept; b_j' $(j = 1,...,5)$ are coefficients for prices, net income, and financial balance; and u' is the error term to be estimated.

C.3.1 *Dynamic income effects*

In dynamic equations the current income effect on demand for land is replaced by a total income effect. In equation [14a], equating the marginal expenditure on land to the real price of land $(E_h=h/p)$ provides

[14a'] $Q_h - \pounds \cdot (E_h \quad dB/dH) = 0.$

Rearranging these terms yields:

[17] $dH/dB - -1 / (Q_h/\pounds \quad h/p)$
given that $\pounds > 0$, and $Q_h/\pounds \lessgtr h/p$.

This *portfolio/productivity condition* has important implications for analyzing farmers' demand for land. It states that financial balance (B) has its own impact on demand for land (H) and that this impact (dH/dB) varies with a farmer's productivity *and* portfolio.

If farmers are insolvent (dB > 0), they are net borrowers, net disinvestors, or both. If productivity keeps up with land prices $(Q_h/\pounds > h/p)$, the balance effect will be negative (dH/dB < 0). If productivity does not keep up with land prices $(Q_h/\pounds < h/p)$, the balance effect will be positive (dH/dB > 0).

If farmers are solvent (dB < 0), they are net savers, net repayers, or both. If productivity keeps up with land prices $(Q_h/\pounds > h/p)$, the balance effect will

where a_0' is the intercept, a_j' (j = 1,...,6) are the coefficients for pri
for each income component, and v' is the error term to be estimated

C.2.1 *Static income and price effects*

If there are few technical discontinuities in agriculture and if econon
scale are not significant, it is expected that demand for land should ris
income. That is, there should be a positive income effect for net in
$(H_Y = a_4 > 0)$ and its components: agricultural, nonagricultural, and si
tence incomes $(H_A' = a_4' > 0, H_N' = a_5' > 0, H_S' = a_6' > 0)$. An increase in
prices, however, has both a substitution and an income effect. The si
tution effect is always negative—an increase in the price of land decr
the demand for land—other things held constant. This effect shoul
enhanced by the positive income effect, since a decrease in income (
voked by the increase in prices) decreases the demand for land. The
own-price effect is thus expected to be negative.

Cross-price effects depend on whether land substitutes for or com
ments other factors. If it is a substitute the cross-price effect shoul
positive $(a_2', a_3' > 0)$. An increase in the wage rate, for example, sh
decrease demand for labor and increase demand for land. But given
opportunity cost of family labor in the outside labor market, an increas
the wage rate beyond the marginal value product of labor on the farm r
discourage household labor, promote exit from farming, and reduce
demand for land. In this case the cross-price effect of wages on demand
land will be negative. Cross-price effects cannot be predicted because tl
generally depend on internal rates of technical substitution between fact
and on farmers' alternatives in the market.

C.3 The Dynamic Model: Indebtedness and Investment

Since equilibrium is rarely attained even under normal circumstances, t
instability of frontier conditions should lead not to equalities (equation [9
but to Kuhn-Tucker inequalities. These inequalities, in turn, require sla
variables to satisfy first-order conditions. By relaxing conditions (equatic
[8]), surplus or deficit arises in current accounts, with the balance in financi
account (B) picking up the slack, (B = D − I) becomes the slack variable i
the model. Thus, equation [9] becomes:

[14] a) $Q_i - \pounds \cdot (E_i - B_i) = 0$
        where $Q_i = dQ/di$ is the marginal productivity of factor i = L,C,H,
        as in [9]; $E_i = dE/di$ is the marginal expenditure on factor i;
        $B_i = D_i - I_i = 0$ is the effect of factor i on balance of financial
        account; $\pounds$ is a Lagrangean multiplier.
    b) Y + B = 0.

be positive (dH/dB > 0). If productivity does not keep up with land prices ($Q_h/\pounds$ < h/p), the balance effect will be negative (dH/dB < 0).

Table C.1 presents a summary of these cases.

Table C.1 Dynamic Income Effects: Productivity and Portfolio

Productivity	Portfolio	
	Solvent: dB < 0	*Insolvent: dB > 0*
Productive: Q_h > h/p	dH/dB > 0	dH/dB < 0
Unproductive: Q_h < h/p	dH/dB < 0	dH/dB > 0

Case 1. Among solvent farmers (dB < 0) whose productivity is keeping up with real land prices (Q_h > h/p), the dynamic effect should be positive, adding to the static income effect. The total income effect should be relatively large and positive.

Case 2. Among solvent farmers (dB < 0) whose productivity is not keeping up with real land prices (Q_h < h/p), the dynamic effect should be negative, reducing the static income effect. The total income effect may be positive, though relatively small, or even negative. Increasing incomes are directed out of agriculture and land is held as a store of value, rather than as a factor of production.

Case 3. Among insolvent farmers (dB > 0) whose productivity is keeping up with real land prices (Q_h > h/p), the dynamic effect should be negative, reducing the static income effect. The total income effect may be positive, though relatively small, or even negative. Agricultural product is being used to pay off debt, so increasing incomes are directed out of agriculture. Land is held as a store of value rather than as a factor of production.

Case 4. Among insolvent farmers (dB > 0) whose productivity is not keeping up with real land prices (Q_h < h/p), the dynamic effect should be positive, adding to the static income effect. The total income effect will be relatively large and positive. This is an example of debt peonage, where farmers over-work their own families and land to pay off debt.

C.3.2 Dynamic price effects

The effect of own-price variation on demand for land is expected to contain two components: a negative substitution effect (dH/d[h/p] < 0) and an income effect, which may be static or dynamic. The static income effect (dH/dY > 0) is expected to be positive. The dynamic effect may be larger or smaller than the static income effect (dH/dTY $\lessgtr$ dH/dY) according to portfolio and productivity (see table C.1). The total income effect can be negative under extreme conditions (special cases of 2 and 3, above).

If the income effect is positive, the total own-price effect should be negative—as prices rise, demand falls. But if the income effect is negative, it dampens the price effect and may provoke a positive own-price effect. A positive own-price effect on the demand for land would arise if productive farmers become increasingly insolvent or if the productivity of solvent farmers does not keep up with rising land prices.

The overall effect of land price on demand for land cannot be predicted. A negative overall own-price effect may be a *solvent/productive* (case 1) or an *insolvent/unproductive* (case 4) response to land price. Either can be called a *productive response* to land price variation. A perverse, positive, overall own-price effect may be an *insolvent/productive* (case 2) or a *solvent/unproductive* (case 3) response to land price. Either of the two may be called a *speculative response* to land price variation.

C.4 Empirical Equations

The empirical equations derived from the model regress total deforested area (F) against real prices for land (h/p), labor (w/p), other costs (c/p), and an income variable. This income variable is specified differently according to each version of the model. The static model uses current income (Y) or its income components—agricultural (A), nonagricultural (N), or subsistence (S). The dynamic model uses total income (TY) or total income components: net indebtedness (D) and net investment (I).

The four regressions (estimated in appendix D) are derived from equations [12] and [16], as follows:

Static model:

[1] $F = a_0 + a_1 \cdot h/p + a_2 \cdot w/p + a_3 \cdot c/p + a_4 \cdot Y + v.$

2] $F = a_0' + a_1' \cdot h/p + a_2' \cdot w/p + a_3' \cdot c/p + a_4' \cdot A + a_5' \cdot N + a_6' \cdot S + v'.$

Dynamic model:

3] $F = b_0 + b_1 \cdot h/p + b_2 \cdot w/p + b_3 \cdot c/p + b_4 \cdot TY + u.$

[4] $F = b_0' + b_1' \cdot h/p + b_2' \cdot w/p + b_3' \cdot c/p + b_4' \cdot Y + b_5' \cdot B + u'$

where a_0 and b_0 are intercepts; a_j ($j = 1,...,4$), a_j' ($j = 1,...,6$), b_j ($j = 1,...,4$), and b_j' ($j = 1,...,5$) are coefficients; and v, v', u, and u' are the error terms to be estimated.

If the income effect is positive, income coefficient estimates are expected to be positive:

Static model:

[1] $a_4 > 0$.

[2] $a_j' > 0$ (j = 4,5,6).

Dynamic model:

[3] $b_4 > 0$.

[4] $b_j' > 0$ (j = 4,5).

The total own-price effect on demand for land should be negative, and all land-price coefficient estimates are expected to be negative:

Static model:

[1] $a_1 < 0$.

[2] $a_1' < 0$.

Dynamic model:

[3] $b_1 < 0$.

[4] $b_1' < 0$.

It the income effect is negative, it may provoke a positive own-price effect on the demand for land. Expected coefficient estimates then are opposite in sign from those above. According to table C.1, this would be the case if productive farmers become increasingly indebted or if the productivity of solvent farmers does not keep up with rising land prices.

The overall effect of land price variation on demand for land cannot be predicted. A negative overall own-price effect may be called a *productive response* to land price variation. A positive overall own-price effect may be called a *speculative response* to land price variation.

C.5 Summary and Policy Implications

The previous sections propose that frontier farmers deforest differently in response to changes in income and land prices according to whether they are productive in agriculture (productive response) or speculating in the land market (speculative response).

A *productive response* occurs when farmers are solvent and land is productive (table C.1, case 1) or when farmers are insolvent and land is unproductive (table C.1, case 4). In the first case, farmers with relatively high rates of accumulation respond to rising incomes by increasing demand for land, and they respond to rising land prices by decreasing demand for land. In the second case, debt peonage occurs. Farmers also respond to rising incomes by increasing their demand for land. Their response to rising prices is a decreased demand for land.

A *speculative response* occurs when farmers are solvent and land is unproductive (table C.1, case 2) or when farmers are insolvent and land is productive (table C.1, case 3). In case 2, low yields drive farmers out of agriculture so that rising incomes may decrease demand for land while rising land prices may increase demand for land. In case 3, it is debt that drives farmers out of agriculture, but the effects of rising incomes on demand for land are the same as in case 2.

In agricultural frontier economies, deforestation can be taken as a form of demand for land. Such demand may be for productive purposes—which would imply productive deforestation—or for speculative purposes, which would imply speculative deforestation. Farmers who are deforesting for the purpose of agricultural production are sensitive to price and income variations. On the other hand, farmers who deforest in order to hold land as a store of value respond inversely to variations in prices and incomes. Economic policies intended for agriculturally productive farmers would only reinforce speculative farmers' motives for holding land. Policies aimed at raising the level of sustainability of small Amazonian farming must, therefore, determine which motive—that is, production or speculation—prevails in a specific frontier.

This model's empirical equations are estimated according to the statistical procedures outlined in appendix D.

Notes

1. This procedure disregards a vast discussion in the literature on how to analyze the cost of household labor in family farming or peasant agriculture, referred to in FAO/INCRA (1992).

2. See Ozório de Almeida (1991b) for literature on, and modeling of, debt peonage in the Amazon frontier.

3. The rate of accumulation, time on plot, and initial capital are included in the econometric model tested in appendix D.

4. Chapter 4 confirmed these predictions by showing that the frontier locations with the highest rates of accumulation were those where agriculture was most productive and where agricultural income accounted for the highest shares of total income.

APPENDIX D

Econometric Results

Estimation of the Model

Theoretical variables

Given the data base described in appendix B, translating the theoretical model in appendix C into quantifiable variables requires adjustments. The principal variables were observed in many different ways, and more empirical tests were performed than reported.

Deforestation was observed since farmers' arrival (F) and during the current agricultural year (F91).[1] Income was measured as current total gross income (GY) or its components—gross agricultural (A), net nonagricultural (N), and net subsistence (S) incomes. Net income (Y) is gross income minus current agricultural production expenditures (E). Total income (TY) is gross income (GY) plus balance on financial account (B), which is composed of net indebtedness (D) minus net investment (I). Price of land (h/p) is measured as a weighted average of the value of areas—forested, temporary crop, perennial crop, pasture, fallow, and unproductive. Real wages (w) are measured as an average of daily wages paid to outside workers. Other costs—total (C) and per unit (c/p)—were omitted from the regressions because the composition of inputs varied too much by location and by farmer to permit a viable index.[2] The output price was the average sale price of a kilogram of rice.[3]

Theoretical equations

The model's four empirical equations lead to eight regressions:

Regression:	1	2	3	4
Empirical equation:	[12]	[13]	[15]	[16]
Dependent variables: F, F91				
Constants:	a_0	a_0'	b_0	b_0'
Error terms:	v	v'	u	u'
Independent variables		Coeffi	cients	
Prices: $h/p, w/p$ $(i = 1,2)$	a_i	a_i'	b_i	b_i'
Income: GY	a_4			
A, N, S $(i = 4,5,6)$		a_i'		
Total TY income			b_4	
GY, B $(i = 4,5)$				b_i'

For each dependent variable (F, F91), regression 1 estimates demand for deforestation based on current income (Y) and real price effects. Regression 2 distinguishes agricultural (A) and other activities (N,S) in the current income effect. Regression 3 estimates demand for deforestation based on the total income effect (TY) and price effects. Regression 4 distinguishes indebtedness and investment (B = D − I) in the total income effect.

Shifter variables

If the model was perfectly specified, the above relationships would account for variations in deforestation demand (F, F91) among frontier farmers. But there are many influences on migrant farmer behavior—based on origin, destination, and individual characteristics—that have not been taken into account in this model. Given the lack of information on Amazon colonization, it is important to explore a wider spectrum of possibilities than can be dealt with in a microeconomic hypothesis.

To bring the model into the Amazonian context, several variables were added to regressions 1 to 4. Listed in appendix B, these variables are grouped according to the origin, destination, and individual characteristics of frontier farmers.

Origin characteristics relate to the past: where a farmer comes from (ORIG); whether he was a landowner before (FORM); how itinerant he was (ITIN); whether his parents were farmers (PARNT).

Destination characteristics pertain to conditions since arrival at the frontier, such as:

the kind of a project the farmer participates in: 0 = public (Pará); 1 = private (Mato Grosso) (STAT).

marketing conditions: distance to market (DIST),[4] how much the farmer
   sells at the farm gate (GATE), and how much he sells during the three
   months after harvest (STOR).
the productivity of the land (QH).
tenure: squatter (SQUAT), sharecropper (SCROP), owner (OWN), or titled
   owner (TD).
access to credit (CREDIT) and participation in local institutions—rural
   extension, cooperatives, unions, associations, and church (INST).

Individual characteristics may be personal and family characteristics, or
they may indicate attitudes, perceptions, and expectations. Among the
variables tested are: age (AGE), time on plot (TIME), number of family
workers (WKRS), practice of crop or area rotation (AGCON), perception that
loss of soil fertility may be a problem now or in the future (FERT), belief that
living standard has improved since arrival (IMPR), intention to remain on
plot (FIX), and plans to invest in agriculture (PLAN).

These variables contribute to a farmer's performance. Specifically, a
farmer's deforestation responses to price and income variations may shift
according to scales of origin, destination, or individuality. If so, controlling
these shifts will improve estimation of the productive deforestation model.

Given the complexity of how such influences affect behavior, they are
investigated in a preliminary manner, as indicated below.

Empirical results for the deforestation model are summarized in tables
D.1 and D.2. These tables do not present the estimates themselves (which
are in tables D.3 to D.10)—only the signs of estimates of income and price
coefficients.

The tables also show the percentage contribution and significance of four
estimation steps that reduce residual variation in deforestation. Step 1 is the
deforestation model, step 2 is the origin variables, step 3 is the destination
variables, and step 4 is the individual variables. A letter exponent indicates
the significance of each estimate according to the *F-test*; if there is no letter
exponent, the estimate was not significant at the 10 percent level. Tables
D.3 to D.10 are final (step 4) regressions, with all shifter variables included
for each dependent variable:

   F: deforestation since arrival (tables D.3 to D.6);
   F91: deforestation during 1991 (tables D.7 to D.10).

Analysis of Cross-section Data

Ordinary least squares regressions for deforestation since arrival (F) and
during 1991 (F91) are estimated in the following sequence:

Step 1 estimates coefficients for regressions 1 to 4 (empirical equations [12], [13], [15], and [16]) and tests for the significance of each independent variable. This step also calculates the significance of the deforestation model in reducing the residual variance of dependent variables. All the regressions are included in step 1.

Step 2 also estimates coefficients for variables in step 1, adding origin variables to the regressions. It tests the significance of each origin variable and the joint contribution of the origin variables in reducing residual variance.

Step 3 estimates coefficients for the variables in step 2, adding destination variables to the regressions. It tests the significance of each destination variable and the joint contribution of the destination variables in reducing residual variance.

Step 4 estimates coefficients for the variables in step 3, adding individual variables to the regressions. It tests the significance of each individual variable and the joint contribution of the individual variables in reducing residual variance.

There are thirty-two regressions—eight in each of the four steps.

This procedure controls which variables enter each regression and does not leave the statistical package to determine which variables will be analyzed. The part of the analysis that corresponds to the theoretical model is in step 1. The part of the analysis that is not based on microeconomic modeling is in steps 2, 3, and 4. Steps 2, 3, and 4 introduce *shifter* variables, which change the model's n-space, correcting distortions and omissions not adequately predicted in the theory. In this way, one is rigorous where allowed for and adventurous where possible.

These procedures contain several limitations. No attempt is made to specify the functional form in which the shifter variables enter the equations, linearity being assumed throughout. Steps 2 to 4 are prone to heteroschedasticity, colinearity, excluded variable bias, wrong-specification bias, errors in variables, simultaneity, problems in the use of dummy variables, and the difficulties of regressions based on cross sections.[5] These problems are caused by the exploratory nature of the exercise and the need to attain a set of descriptive results before investing in more sophisticated modeling and statistical analysis.

Empirical Results

This section analyzes regression results for deforestation (F). These regressions correspond to step 1 (model), step 2 (model + origin), step 3 (model + origin + destination), and step 4 (model + origin + destination + individual variables). Step 4 coefficients have signs that are closer to theoretical expectations than step 1 coefficients but tend to display less statistical significance than those of step 1.

Deforestation responds to a large number of influences not accounted for in any single microeconomic model. Excluded variable problems tend to bias theoretical coefficient estimates. Because the signs of these coefficients are crucial to interpreting empirical results, excluded variables are an important problem in the model.

When the inclusion of a variable changes coefficient estimates, this indicates that previous estimates were biased by the omission of important variables. The inclusion is beneficial to the interpretation of results. When the inclusion of a variable does not alter coefficient estimates, estimates of standard errors become upwardly biased. This reduces the significance of theoretical variables. Prior modeling provides expectations regarding the signs of theoretical coefficients. Thus, to draw implications, maximizing statistical significance is less important than minimizing coefficient biases. In other words, the cost of exclusion is high in terms of biased coefficient estimates; the cost of inclusion is low in terms of statistical significance. In this case, too many variables are better than too few.

Two other costs of inclusion should be mentioned. First, missing values are different across observations for each variable; so the larger the number of variables analyzed, the smaller the portion of the total sample used in the regressions. This further reduces the statistical significance of the estimates. Second, simultaneities among many destination and individual variables (steps 3 and 4) and theoretical variables (step 1) provoke an upward bias in R^2 estimates for steps 3 and 4 relative to steps 1 and 2.

For expediency, shorthand terms are used to describe regression results. An estimate is significant if it passes the *t-test* (for an individual coefficient) or the *F-test* (for the group of coefficients estimated in a particular step) at the 10 percent level. The term "explanatory power" is used in reference to reductions in the sum of squared residuals. A coefficient is referred to as the impact of an independent variable on a dependent variable, though causality cannot be inferred from correlation. Other liberties are taken with statistical terminology to facilitate exposition.

Because of space limitations, the coefficients estimated in steps 2 and 3 are omitted from tables D.3 to D.10. Only those obtained in steps 1 and 4 are presented. The analysis of covariance at the foot of each table indicates the statistical significance of each step (1, 2, 3, and 4) in reducing the residual variance in deforestation and displays their respective contributions to R^2.

Analysis of deforestation since arrival

The economic model of deforestation (F—step 1) contributes more than half the reduction in residual variation of deforestation (table D.1). All income effects are significant and positive. Of these, agricultural income is the largest deforester (table D.4). Balance on financial account has a positive income effect (table D.6). This means that solvent, high-productivity farm-

Table D.1 Deforestation Since Arrival
Dependent variable: F

Regression	Static model		Dynamic model	
	1	2	3	4
Empirical equation	[12]	[13]	[15]	[16]
Independent variables	Signs of coefficients			
Prices h/p	+	+	+	+
w/p	$+^b$	+	$+^b$	$+^c$
Income GY	$+^a$			
A		$+^a$		
N		$+^a$		
S		+		
Total income TY	$+^a$			
GY				$+^a$
B				$+^a$
R^2 Step 1: Model	0.42^a	0.72^a	0.53^a	0.61^a
Step 2: Origin	0.13^a	0.14^a	0.14^a	0.14^b
Step 3: Destination	0.15^b	0.03	0.04	0.07
Step 4: Individual	0.01	0.01	0.01	0.06
Total	0.71	0.90	0.72	0.81

Statistical significance tests: a—1 percent; b—5 percent; c—10 percent. The absence of a superscript indicates that the variable is not significant at the 10 percent level.

ers are deforesting to invest in agriculture, while insolvent, low-productivity farmers are deforesting to repay debt (table D.1).

Cross-price effects are positive and generally significant. Contrary to expectation, the effect of the price of land is positive and insignificant. This means that deforestation is not behaving according to a model demand for land. A positive own-price effect was expected only in the case of negative income effects. But all income effects turned out to be positive and significant for total deforestation (F). So the positive impact of land price on deforestation is inconsistent with a productive, current demand response. Farmers are deforesting not to increase agricultural production but to add to their net worth. Therefore, the higher the price of land, the more surrounding lots they purchase and deforest.

The shifter variables are too colinear to attain statistical significance individually. In groups, only origin characteristics (step 2) have a considerable and significant contribution—about 14 percent—to reducing residual variance in deforestation. Of these, prior itinerancy (ITIN) has the most positive effect. Although destination variables are generally insignificant, distance to market (DIST), access to credit (CREDIT), and institutional participation (INST) seem to have positive impacts on deforestation.

Table D.2 Deforestation in 1991

Dependent Variable: F91

Regression	Static Model		Dynamic Model	
	1	2	3	4
Empirical equation	[12]	[13]	[15]	[16]
Independent variables	Signs of coefficients			
Prices h/p	+^{a}	+	+^{a}	+^{a}
w/p	—	—	—	—
Income GY	—			
A		+^{a}		
N		—		
S		—^{a}		
Total income TY			—	
GY				—
B				—
R^2 Step 1: Model	0.33^a	0.73^a	0.31^a	0.35^a
Step 2: Origin	0.14^a	0.14^a	0.14^a	0.15^b
Step 3: Destination	0.24^a	0.04^c	0.27^a	0.23^a
Step 4: Individual	0.01	0.01	0.01	0.01
Total:	0.74	0.92	0.73	0.74

Statistical significance tests: a—1 percent; b—5 percent, c—10 percent. The absence of a superscript indicates that the variable is not significant at the 10 percent level.

Table D.2 indicates that the economic model (step 1) contributed between one-third and two-thirds of the residual variance reduction in deforestation in current year (1991). Agriculture is the most significant deforester—its separation from total income raises the explanatory power of the regression considerably (table D.8), as it did in the case of total deforestation (F). Except for the impact of agricultural income (A), which continues to be positive, all other coefficients change signs. These regressions indicate an important difference in the economic determination of current deforestation (F91) compared with deforestation since arrival (F).

Income effects are negative but generally insignificant. This is the opposite of the finding regarding deforestation since arrival (F) (tables D.3 to D.6), where all income effects were positive and significant. The impact of balance on financial account also switches sign, from positive and significant to negative and insignificant (regression 4, table D.10). This implies that insolvent, high-productivity farmers have large debt burdens and, therefore, have insufficient funds to invest in agriculture. Solvent, low-productivity farmers are diversifying and investing outside of agriculture.

Cross-price effects also switch signs relative to regressions reported in table D.1, becoming negative though insignificant. The effect of land pricing, however, is positive and becomes generally significant. Given the negative income effects for F91, this positive own-price response for F91 is consistent with the economic model of deforestation. It implies that farmers are moving out of agriculture and that a reduction in land price will speed the movement away from agricultural production. This agricultural involution is compounded by dynamic income effects (regressions 3 and 4, tables D.9 and D.10), which are also negative. Thus, farmers who are investing and those that are servicing large debts will move out of agriculture even more quickly when land prices fall.

As before, shifter variables are too colinear to attain statistical significance individually. However, their group contribution is significant in reducing the unexplained variance in current deforestation. After the modeling variables (step 1), destination variables (step 3) are the most important group, contributing about one-quarter of the explanatory power of the regressions. Of these, access to credit is the largest and most significant deforester, followed by participation in local institutions. Being in a public project, selling at the farm gate, and lacking storage have significantly negative impacts. These are probably capturing disguised income effects, since poorer farmers deforest less.

The other two groups of variables—origin and individual—do not attain statistical significance individually. Origin variables are significant as a group and contribute about the same—14 percent—to explaining current deforestation (F91) as they did to deforestation since arrival (F). Thus, total deforestation responds more to origin influences, while current deforestation responds more to destination conditions. Over time, the impact of the past weakens and that of the present grows. It may take time to influence colonists' behavior. Policies do influence migrants, but colonists, particularly recent arrivals, may be insensitive to current stimuli and react to past experiences.[6]

Regression Results

Table D.3 Regression 1: Deforestation (F), Static Model, Aggregate Income

Variable	Parameter estimate	Standard error	F	Prob > F
Intercept	1,991.899	5,286.368	0.14	0.708
Group: Model and origin			8.06	0.000
GY	0.000	0.000	27.65	0.000
h/p	0.113	0.225	0.26	0.615
w/p	1.811	0.767	5.57	0.023
PARNT	29.266	81.761	0.13	0.722
ITIN	23.109	12.952	3.18	0.082
FORM	1.275	53.375	0.00	0.981
ORIG	1.233	62.371	0.00	0.984
Group: Destination			2.28	0.047
STAT	-39.397	86.027	0.21	0.649
DIST3	1.753	0.964	3.30	0.076
QH	0.000	0.000	0.00	0.993
STOR	31.403	68.104	0.21	0.647
GATE	-95.562	63.069	2.30	0.137
INST	46.339	22.295	4.32	0.044
CREDIT	214.816	118.185	3.30	0.076
Group: Individual			0.23	0.963
TIME	0.060	0.509	0.01	0.905
K_0	0.000	0.001	0.10	0.748
AGE	-1.663	2.046	0.66	0.421
TD	-49.337	86.323	0.33	0.570
AGCON	25.591	82.459	0.10	0.757
FERT	-34.276	57.032	0.36	0.551

Summary of Stepwise Procedure for Dependent Variable F

Step	Group entered	Number	Partial R^2	Model R^2	C(p)	F	Prob > F
1	Model	3	0.4200				
2	Origin	7	0.1300	0.5504	18.0856	9.27	0.001
3	Destination	14	0.1546	0.7050	10.3902	3.4445	0.0048
4	Individual	20	0.0099	0.7149	21.0000	0.2317	0.9638

Table D.4 Regression 2: Deforestation (F), Static Model, Disaggregated Income

Variable	Parameter estimate	Standard error	F	Prob > F
Intercept	-24.088	3,446.480	0.00	0.994
Group: Model and origin			23.85	0.000
A	0.006	0.001	15.19	0.000
N	0.000	0.000	10.00	0.003
S	0.001	0.001	1.32	0.257
h/p	0.059	0.155	0.14	0.706
w/p	0.237	0.510	0.22	0.644
PARNT	9.871	50.617	0.04	0.846
ITIN	4.737	8.318	0.32	0.572
FORM	4.977	33.024	0.02	0.881
ORIG	26.158	39.162	0.45	0.508
Group: Destination			0.99	0.454
STAT	-8.753	56.442	0.02	0.877
DIST3	0.982	0.603	2.65	0.112
QH	0.000	0.000	0.41	0.526
STOR	-2.935	42.348	0.00	0.945
GATE	-36.915	40.125	0.85	0.363
INST	16.501	14.839	1.25	0.270
CREDIT	-61.426	125.582	0.24	0.627
Group: Individual			0.86	0.529
TIME	-0.071	0.314	0.05	0.822
K_0	0.001	0.000	1.91	0.175
AGE	-0.070	1.295	0.00	0.956
TD	-93.889	53.638	3.06	0.088
AGCON	5.453	51.057	0.01	0.915
FERT	-3.651	35.458	0.01	0.918

Summary of Stepwise Procedure for Dependent Variable F

Step	Group entered	Number	Partial R^2	Model R^2	C(p)	F	Prob > F
1	Model	5	0.7200				
2	Origin	9	0.1400	0.8487	14.6066	31.81	0.0001
3	Destination	16	0.0338	0.8826	16.1840	1.8081	0.1097
4	Individual	22	0.0141	0.8967	23.0000	0.8641	0.5299

Table D.5 Regression 3: Deforestation (F), Dynamic Model, Aggregate Income

Variable	Parameter estimate	Standard error	F	Prob > F
Intercept	-4,873.952	5,242.006	0.86	0.358
Group: Model and origin			0.52	0.000
TY	0.002	0.000	29.95	0.000
h/p	0.034	0.222	0.02	0.876
w/p	1.567	0.766	4.18	0.047
PARNT	-43.633	80.875	0.29	0.592
ITIN	16.401	12.943	1.61	0.212
FORM	30.414	51.822	0.34	0.560
ORIG	58.381	62.305	0.88	0.354
Group: Destination			0.67	0.697
STAT	72.588	84.933	0.73	0.397
DIST3	-0.429	1.050	0.17	0.684
QH	0.000	0.000	0.26	0.614
STOR	39.459	66.834	0.35	0.558
GATE	-25.038	62.353	0.16	0.690
INST	10.701	22.586	0.22	0.638
CREDIT	83.746	118.223	0.50	0.482
Group: Individual			0.32	0.923
TIME	-0.212	0.503	0.18	0.675
K_0	0.000	0.001	0.08	0.775
AGE	0.145	2.056	0.01	0.943
TD	-49.485	84.893	0.34	0.563
AGCON	-34.712	81.824	0.18	0.673
FERT	-30.324	55.940	0.47	0.497

Summary of Stepwise Procedure for Dependent Variable F

Step	Group entered	Number	Partial R^2	Model R^2	C(p)	F	Prob > F
1	Model	3	0.5300				
2	Origin	7	0.1400	0.6627	3.9311	14.04	0.001
3	Destination	14	0.0484	0.7111	10.9084	1.1013	0.3784
4	Individual	20	0.0132	0.7243	21.0000	0.3181	0.9237

Table D.6 Regression 4: Deforestation (F), Dynamic Model, Disaggregated Income

Variable	Parameter estimate	Standard error	F	Prob > F
Intercept	-1,950.979	4,495.922	0.19	0.666
Group: Model and origin			12.50	0.000
GY	0.001	0.000	30.71	0.000
B	0.001	0.000	18.68	0.000
h/p	0.015	0.188	0.01	0.933
w/p	1.180	0.655	3.24	0.079
PARNT	-14.772	68.847	0.05	0.831
ITIN	14.438	10.971	1.73	0.195
FORM	1.426	44.449	0.00	0.974
ORIG	44.032	52.877	0.69	0.410
Group: Destination			1.12	0.371
STAT	21.277	73.004	0.08	0.772
DIST3	0.032	0.896	0.00	0.971
QH	0.000	0.000	0.17	0.682
STOR	21.823	56.759	0.15	0.702
GATE	-55.666	53.327	1.09	0.303
INST	22.763	19.352	1.38	0.246
CREDIT	124.658	100.608	1.54	0.222
Group: Individual			0.20	0.975
TIME	-0.141	0.426	0.11	0.741
K_0	0.000	0.001	0.08	0.775
AGE	-0.095	1.742	0.00	0.956
TD	-55.937	71.905	0.61	0.441
AGCON	-18.032	69.408	0.07	0.796
FERT	-15.948	47.684	0.11	0.739

Summary of Stepwise Procedure for Dependent Variable F

Step	Group entered	Number	Partial R^2	Model R^2	C(p)	F	Prob > F
1	Model	4	0.6100				
2	Origin	8	0.1400	0.7365	10.2986	12.50	0.0001
3	Destination	15	0.0648	0.8014	11.1854	2.0978	0.0632
4	Individual	21	0.0059	0.8072	22.0000	0.1976	0.9756

Table D.7 Regression 1: Deforestation (F91), Static Model, Aggregate Income

Variable	Parameter estimate	Standard error	F	Prob > F
Intercept	11,347.177	4,302.804	6.95	0.013
Group: Model and origin			3.88	0.004
GY	0.000	0.000	0.28	0.602
h/p	0.869	0.172	25.54	0.000
w/p	-0.594	0.546	1.18	0.285
PARNT	-10.427	58.335	0.03	0.859
ITIN	3.296	9.809	0.11	0.739
FORM	27.314	47.306	0.33	0.568
ORIG	-12.588	45.054	0.08	0.781
Group: Destination			3.96	0.003
STAT	-218.502	72.523	93.08	0.005
DIST3	0.282	0.695	0.17	0.687
QH	0.000	0.000	0.25	0.620
STOR	-66.228	55.975	1.40	0.246
GATE	-93.543	51.582	3.29	0.080
INST	36.592	16.271	5.06	0.032
CREDIT	275.072	83.574	10.83	0.002
Group: Individual			0.21	0.971
TIME	0.227	0.362	0.39	0.534
K_0	0.000	0.001	0.12	0.729
AGE	0.263	1.552	0.03	0.866
TD	19.559	67.813	0.08	0.775
AGCON	47.100	73.834	0.41	0.528
FERT	-7.827	46.002	0.03	0.866

Summary of Stepwise Procedure for Dependent Variable F91

Step	Group entered	Number	Partial R^2	Model R^2	$C(p)$	F	Prob > F
1	Model	3	0.3300				
2	Origin	7	0.1400	0.4799	24.0960	5.54	0.0001
3	Destination	14	0.2493	0.7293	10.2422	4.6051	0.0010
4	Individual	20	0.0111	0.7404	21.0000	0.2070	0.9718

Table D.8 Regression 2: Deforestation (F91), Static Model, Disaggregated Income

Variable	Parameter estimate	Standard error	F	Prob > F
Intercept	777.196	2,893.684	0.07	0.790
Group: Model and origin			15.96	0.000
A	0.007	0.001	48.54	0.000
N	0.000	0.000	0.20	0.656
S	-0.008	0.001	61.62	0.000
h/p	0.187	0.135	1.93	0.176
w/p	-0.099	0.324	0.09	0.761
PARNT	22.277	34.008	0.43	0.518
ITIN	-1.298	6.017	0.05	0.830
FORM	23.215	27.193	0.73	0.400
ORIG	29.589	26.930	1.21	0.281
Group: Destination			1.51	0.205
STAT	-30.018	49.274	0.37	0.547
DIST3	0.404	0.399	1.02	0.320
QH	0.000	0.000	0.32	0.574
STOR	-12.483	32.907	0.14	0.707
GATE	-0.807	34.682	0.00	0.981
INST	8.502	10.445	0.66	0.422
CREDIT	-130.716	71.716	3.32	0.079
Group: Individual			0.43	0.854
TIME	0.077	0.210	0.13	0.717
K_0	0.000	0.000	0.94	0.340
AGE	0.597	0.954	0.39	0.536
TD	-9.743	39.820	0.06	0.808
AGCON	13.128	43.061	0.09	0.762
FERT	27.126	27.668	0.96	0.335

Summary of Stepwise Procedure for Dependent Variable F91

Step	Group entered	Number	Partial R^2	Model R^2	C(p)	F	Prob > F
1	Model	5	0.7300				
2	Origin	9	0.1400	0.8724	13.3096	30.3969	0.0001
3	Destination	16	0.0405	0.9129	13.5574	2.1934	0.0606
4	Individual	22	0.0075	0.9205	23.0000	0.4262	0.8549

Table D.9 Regression 3: Deforestation (F91), Dynamic Model, Aggregate Income

Variable	Parameter estimate	Standard error	F	Prob > F
Intercept	12,117.644	4,287.165	7.99	0.008
Group: Model and origin			3.86	0.004
TY	0.000	0.000	0.20	0.661
h/p	0.873	0.174	24.99	0.000
w/p	-0.612	0.544	1.27	0.269
PARNT	-4.721	58.735	0.01	0.936
ITIN	3.301	9.898	0.11	0.741
FORM	20.524	44.255	0.22	0.646
ORIG	-17.952	46.035	0.15	0.699
Group: Destination			4.30	0.002
STAT	-231.297	71.788	10.38	0.003
DIST3	0.391	0.762	0.26	0.611
QH	0.000	0.000	0.34	0.566
STOR	-66.969	55.994	1.43	0.241
GATE	-101.131	51.515	3.85	0.059
INST	39.611	16.803	5.56	0.025
CREDIT	281.581	84.341	11.15	0.002
Group: Individual			0.23	0.961
TIME	0.244	0.367	0.44	0.510
K_0	0.000	0.001	0.16	0.696
AGE	0.115	1.615	0.01	0.943
TD	17.772	67.728	0.07	0.794
AGCON	56.544	74.323	0.58	0.452
FERT	-11.055	46.349	0.06	0.813

Summary of Stepwise Procedure for Dependent Variable F91

Step	Group entered	Number	Partial R^2	Model R^2	C(p)	F	Prob > F
1	Model	3	0.3100				
2	Origin	7	0.1400	0.4535	26.8697	4.98	0.0004
3	Destination	14	0.2735	0.7271	10.4037	5.0103	0.0005
4	Individual	20	0.0126	0.7379	21.0000	0.2339	0.9619

Table D.10 Regression 4: Deforestation (F91), Dynamic Model, Disaggregated Income

Variable	Parameter estimate	Standard error	F	Prob > F
Intercept	11,645.663	4,525.022	6.62	0.015
Group: Model and origin			3.29	0.008
GY	0.000	0.000	0.14	0.715
B	0.000	0.000	0.07	0.798
h/p	0.877	0.177	24.39	0.000
w/p	-0.570	0.563	1.03	0.319
PARNT	-7.803	60.168	0.02	0.897
ITIN	3.723	10.108	0.14	0.715
FORM	27.065	48.096	0.32	0.578
ORIG	-15.497	47.172	0.11	0.745
Group: Destination			3.63	0.006
STAT	-223.179	75.927	8.64	0.006
DIST3	0.365	0.777	0.22	0.641
QH	0.000	0.000	0.27	0.605
STOR	-65.471	56.974	1.32	0.260
GATE	-96.508	53.684	3.23	0.083
INST	38.082	17.523	4.72	0.038
CREDIT	278.504	85.994	10.49	0.003
Group: Individual			0.21	0.972
TIME	0.242	0.372	0.42	0.520
K_0	0.000	0.001	0.12	0.735
AGE	0.147	1.641	0.01	0.929
TD	19.690	68.934	0.08	0.777
AGCON	51.210	76.734	0.45	0.510
FERT	-9.518	47.221	0.04	0.841

Summary of Stepwise Procedure for Dependent Variable F91

Step	Group entered	Number	Partial R^2	Model R^2	C(p)	F	Prob > F
1	Model	4	0.3500				
2	Origin	8	0.1500	0.4948	22.6148	5.02	0.0002
3	Destination	15	0.2348	0.7296	11.2325	4.2174	0.0019
4	Individual	21	0.0114	0.7410	22.0000	0.2054	0.9722

Notes

1. Many more dependent variables than those reported here were tested: deforestation during first three years (F3); demand for total land (H); demand for harvested area (FA); time on plot (T); survival from the first survey (in 1981) to the second (in 1991) on the same plot of land (SURV), among other things. Time and resource constraints prevent presentation of the full set of estimates performed. The ones included summarize the main findings and contain the most important implications.

2. An effort was made to include one or two representative cost items, such as fuel, but the cost of doing so, in terms of the number of observations sacrificed, was too great relative to the benefit of including an additional variable in the regressions.

3. Rice is the only crop produced by all farmers in all parts of the frontier. So it was the only possible numéraire. See Ozório de Almeida (1992b, chapter 17) for further evidence of its predominance in the Amazon frontier.

4. Three different measurements of distance were taken (see appendix B). Travel time from local center to plot (DIST3) appeared to be the most sensitive to the estimation procedure.

5. See Ozório de Almeida (1992, chapter 20) for a use of similar methodology and a discussion of the relevant econometric literature.

6. A similar finding is reported in Ozório de Almeida (1992b, chapter 21).

Bibliography

Ahmad, Yusuf J., Salah El Serafy, and Ernst Lutz (eds.). 1989. *Environmental Accounting for Sustainable Development*. Washington, D.C.: World Bank.

Akwabi-Ameyaw. 1990. "The Political Economy of Agricultural Resettlement and Rural Development in Zimbabwe: The Performance of Family Farms and Producer Cooperatives." *Human Organization* 49(4): 320–338.

Alicbusan-Schwab, Adelaida, and John F. Wilson. 1991. "Development Policies and Health: Farmers, Goldminers, and Slums in the Brazilian Amazon." Environment Department Working Paper 1991–18. World Bank, Washington, D.C.

Alston, Lee J., Gary Libecap, and Robert Schneider. Forthcoming. "The Determinants and Impact of Property Rights: Land Titles on the Brazilian Frontier." *Journal of Law, Economics, and Organization*.

Anderson, Anthony B. 1987. "Forest Management Issues in the Brazilian Amazon." Department of Botany, Museu Paraense Emílio Goeldi, Pará, Brazil.

————, ed. 1990. *Alternatives to Deforestation: Steps Toward Sustainable Use of the Amazon Rain Forest*. New York: Columbia University Press.

Anderson, Anthony, and Darrel A. Posey. 1989. "Reflorestamento Indígena." *Ciência Hoje* 6(31): 29–50.

Anderson, Jock R. 1992. "Difficulties in African Agricultural Systems Enhancement— Ten Hypotheses." *Agricultural Systems*, 38: 387–409.

Arrhenius, Eric A., and Thomas W. Waltz. 1990. "The Greenhouse Effect: Implications for Economic Development." Environment Department Discussion Paper 78. World Bank, Washington, D.C.

Ascher, William, and Robert Healy. 1990. *Natural Resource Policymaking in Developing Countries*. Durham, North Carolina: Duke University Press.

Aubertin, C. 1990. "Population Movements and Economic Change in Central Western Brazil." *Cahiers Orstom, Serie Sciences Humanes* 26(3): 327–42.

Bacha, Edmar, and Herbert Klein, eds. 1986. *A Transição Incompleta: Brasil desde 1945*, Vols. 1 and 2. São Paulo: Paz e Terra.

Bakx, Keith. 1987. "Planning Agrarian Reform: Amazonian Settlement Projects, 1970–86." *Development and Change* 18(4): 533–555.

Bank, G., and K. Kooning, eds. 1988. *Social Change in Contemporary Brazil*. Amsterdam: CEDLA.

Barbier, Edward B., Joanne C. Burgess, and others. 1991. "The Economics of Tropical Deforestation." *AMBIO* 20(2): 55–58.

Barbira-Schazzochio, Françoise, ed. 1980. *Land, People and Planning in Contemporary Amazonia*. Occasional Publication 3. Cambridge, U.K.: Centre for Latin American Studies, Cambridge University.

Bardhan, Pranab K. 1984. *Land, Labor, and Rural Poverty: Essays in Development Economics*. New York: Columbia University Press.

Barnes, Douglas F., and José Olivares. 1988. "Sustainable Resource Management in Agriculture and Rural Development Projects: A Review of Bank Policies, Procedures, and Results." Environment Department Working Paper 5. World Bank, Washington, D.C.

Baumol, William, and Wallace Oates. 1988. *The Theory of Environmental Policy*. New York: Cambridge University Press.

Beckerman, Wilfred. 1992. "Economic Growth and the Environment: Whose Growth? Whose Environment?" *World Development* 20(4): 481–496.

Besley, T. 1993. *Property Rights and Investment Incentives: Theory and Micro-evidence from Ghana*. Discussion Paper 170. Research Program in Development Studies. Princeton, N.J.: Princeton University Press.

Bhadra, Dipasis, and Antônio Salazar P. Brandão. 1993. *Urbanization, Agricultural Development, and Land Allocation*. World Bank Discussion Paper 201. Washington, D.C.

Bhattacharya, Rina. 1990. "Common Property Externalities: Isolation, Assurance and Resource Depletion in a Traditional Grazing Context." Environment Department Working Paper 1990-10. World Bank, Washington, D.C.

Bigot, Yves, Hans Binswanger, and others. 1987. *Agricultural Mechanization and the Evolution of Farming Systems in Sub-Saharan Africa*. Baltimore, Md.: Johns Hopkins University Press.

Binswanger, Hans. 1980. "Attitudes Toward Risk: Experimental Measurement in Rural India." *American Journal of Agricultural Economics* (62)3: 395–407.

———. 1994. "Brazilian Policies that Encourage Deforestation in the Amazon." *World Development* 19(7): 821–829.

Binswager, Hans, and John McIntire. 1987. "Behavioral and Material Determinants of Production Relations in Land-Abundant Tropical Agriculture." *Economic Development and Cultural Change* 36(1): 73–99.

Binswanger, Hans P., and Miranda Elgin. 1989. "Quais são as Perspectivas para a Reforma Agrária?" *Pesquisa e Planejamento Econômico* 19(1).

Binswanger, Hans, Klaus Deininger, and Gershon Feder. 1993. "Power, Distortions, Revolt, and Reform in Agricultural Land Relations." In T.N. Srinivasan and Jere Behrman, eds. *Handbook of Development Economics*, Vol. IIIB. Amsterdam: North Holland.

Blount, Jeb. 1993. "40 Yanomami Indians Slain On Brazilian Reservation." *Washington Post*, August 21.

Bonfim, Antulio N., and Anwar Shah. 1991. "Macroeconomic Management and the Division of Powers in Brazil: Perspectives for the Nineties." Working Paper 567. World Bank, Washington, D.C.

Brandão, Antônio Salazar P., and Gervasio Castro de Rezende. 1992. "Credit Subsidies, Inflation and the Land Market in Brazil: A Theoretical and Empirical Analysis." Fundação Getulio Vargas Graduate School of Economics, Rio de Janeiro.

Brito, Maria Socorro, and Mitiko Yanaga Une. 1987. "A Evolução da Agricultura Brasileira na Região Norte na Decada de 70." *Revista Brasileira de Geografia* 49 (January/March) 11–46.

Brito, Maristella de Azevedo. 1987. "Questoes Associadas a Evolução Recente da Agricultura Brasileira," *Revista Brasileira de Geografia* 49 (January/March): 139–161.

Brokensha, David, and Alfonso Peter Castro. 1984. *Fuelwood, Agro-Forestry, and Natural Resource Management-Utilization Systems.* New York: Institute for Development Anthropology.

Brooks, E. 1974. "Frontiers of Ethnic Conflict in the Brazilian Amazon." *International Journal of Environmental Studies* 7: 63–74.

Browder, John. 1988. "Public Policy and Deforestation in the Brazilian Amazon." In Robert Repetto and Malcolm Gillis, eds. *Public Policies and the Misuse of Forest Resources.* Cambridge, U.K.: Cambridge University Press.

———. 1989. *Fragile Lands of Latin America: Strategies for Sustainable Development.* Boulder, Colo.: Westview Press.

Brown, Lawrence, and Douglas Southgate. 1991. "The Causes of Tropical Deforestation in Ecuador." *World Development* 19(9): 1145–1151.

Brown, Nigel. 1990. "Mercury Pollution with Specific Reference to the Amazon Basin." University of London.

Bruneau, Thomas, and Rolf Wesche. 1990. *Integration and Change in Brazil's Middle Amazon.* Ottawa: University of Ottawa Press.

Bunker, Stephen. 1985. *Underdeveloping the Amazon: Extraction, Unequal Exchange and the Failure of the Modern State.* Chicago, Ill.: University of Illinois Press.

Campari, João. 1994. "Ill-Defined and Poorly Enforced Property Rights: A Role for Multilateral Organizations and Local Governments." University of Texas at Austin, Department of Economics, Austin, Texas.

———. 1993a. "First- and Second-Best Policies to Control Deforestation in the Brazilian Amazon." University of Texas at Austin, Department of Economics, Austin, Texas.

———. 1993b. "Liquidity-Constrained Agents and the Sub-Optimal Allocation of Natural Resources." University of Texas at Austin, Department of Economics, Austin, Texas.

Cano, Wilson. 1985. *Desequilíbrios Regionais e Concentração Industrial no Brasil, 1930–1970.* Campinas: Ed. UNICAMP.

de Carvalho, Magno, Jose Alberto, and Charles Wood. 1988. *The Demography of Inequality.* Cambridge, U.K.: Cambridge University Press.

Castro, Antonio. 1980. *Ensaios sobre a Economia Brasileira.* Rio de Janeiro: Forense-Universitária.

Castro de Rezende, Gervásio, and Antonio Salazar Brandão. 1992. "Credit Subsidies, Inflation and the Land Market in Brazil: A Theoretical and Empirical Analysis." Agricultural and Natural Resources Department, World Bank, Washington, D.C.

Cernea, Michael. 1988. *Nongovernmental Organizations and Local Development.* World Bank Discussion Paper 40. Washington, DC.

Chalamwong, Yongyuth, Gershon Feder, and others. 1988. *Land Policies and Farm Productivity in Thailand.* Baltimore, Md.: Johns Hopkins University Press.

Cleary, D. 1991. "The Brazilian Rainforest: Politics, Finance, Mining, and the Environment." *Economist* 2100: 66.

Collins, Jane. 1981. "Kinship and Seasonal Migration Among the Aymara of Southern Peru: Human Adaptation to Energy Scarcity." Unpublished dissertation. University of Florida, Gainesville.

———. 1986. "Smallholder Settlement of Tropical South America: The Social Causes of Ecological Destruction." *Human Organization* 45:1–10.

Dalfelt, Arne. 1991. "Ecological Constraints to Sustainable Management of the Tropical Moist Forest." Environment Department Working Paper 1991–25. World Bank, Washington, DC.

Dalrymple, J. B., and D. M. Robison. 1989. "A Soil-Based Assessment of the Sustainability of a Zero-Input Alternative to Shifting Cultivation in Bolívia." *Interciencia* 14(6):329–40.

Daly, Herman. 1991. "Ecological Economics and Sustainable Development: From Concept to Policy." Environment Department Working Paper 1991–24. World Bank, Washington, DC.

Daly, Herman, Robert Goodland, and others, eds. 1991. "Environmentally Sustainable Economic Development—Building on Brundtland." Environment Department Working Paper 46. World Bank, Washington, DC.

Davis, Shelton H., ed. 1991. *Indigenous Views of Land and the Environment*. Discussion Paper 188. World Bank, Washington, D.C.

Davis, Shelton, and Alaka Wali. 1991. "Land Regularization in Special Amerindian Components of Bank-Funded Projects in Lowland South America." Latin America and Caribbean Department, World Bank, Washington, D.C.

Deacon, Robert. 1990. "Government Policy and Environmental Quality in Developing Countries: Complements or Substitutes?" Department of Economics, University of California, Santa Barbara, Calif.

de Freitas, Davies, and Maria de Lourdes. 1989. "Desmatamento na Amazônia: Causas, Efeitos e Soluções." *Interciencia* 14(6):298–303.

Denevan, W. 1978. "The Causes and Consequences of Shifting Cultivation in Relation to Tropical Forest Survival." In Denevan, W. (ed), *The Role of Geographical Research in Latin America*. Publication 7. Conference of Latin Americanist Geographers.

Dewees, Peter A. 1992. "Tree Planting and Household Decision Making Process Amongst Smallholders in Kenya." Food Studies Group, Oxford University.

Dickenson, J. P. 1989. "Development in Brazilian Amazonia: Background to New Frontiers." *Revista Geográfica* 109: 141–155.

D'Silva, Emmanuel, and Simmathiri Appenah. 1993. *Forestry Management for Sustainable Development*. EDI Seminar Report No. 32. Washington, D.C.: World Bank

Dunham, David. 1989. "Politics and Land Settlement Schemes: The Case of Sri Lanka." *Development and Change* 13(1): 43.

Eastwood, D. A., and H. J. Pollard. 1985. "The Development of Colonization in Lowland Bolivia: Objectives and Evaluation." *Boletin de Estudios Latinoamericanos y del Caribe* 38: 61.

Eden, Michael. 1988. "Crop Diversity in Tropical Swidden Cultivation: Comparative Data From Colombia and Papua New Guinea." *Agriculture, Ecosystems and Environment* 20: 127–136.

———. 1990. *Ecology and Land Management in Amazonia.* New York: Bellhaven Press.

Eggertsson, Thrainn. 1990. *Economic Behavior of Institutions.* New York: Cambridge University Press.

Ehrlich, Anne H., and Paul R. Ehrlich. 1992. "The Value of Biodiversity." *AMBIO* 21(3): 219–243.

Ehui, Simeon K. 1990. "Forest Resource Depletion, Soil Dynamics, and Agricultural Productivity in the Tropics." *Journal of Environmental Economics and Management* 18: 136–154.

Eskeland, Gunnar S., and Emmanuel Jimenez. 1992. "Policy Instruments for Pollution Control in Developing Countries." *World Bank Observer* 7(2): 145–69.

Ewell, Peter T., and Thomas T. Poleman. 1982. "Uxpanapa: Resettlement and Agricultural Development in the Mexican Tropics." *A.E. Research* 82–7.Cornell/International Agricultural Economics Study, Ithaca, N.Y.

Fearnside, Phillip. 1986. *Human Carrying Capacity of the Brazilian Rainforest.* New York: Columbia University Press.

———. 1989. "Deforestation and Agricultural Development in Brazilian Amazonia." *Interciencia* 14(6): 291-97.

———. 1993. "Deforestation in Brazilian Amazonia: The Effects of Population and Land Tenure." *AMBIO* 22(8): 537–45.

Feder, Gershon, and David Feeny. 1991. "Land Tenure and Property Rights: Theory and Implications for Development Policy." *World Bank Economic Review* 5 (January): 135–53.

Feder, Gershon, Tongroj Onchan, Yongyuth Chalamwong, and Chira Honglacharon. 1988. *Land Policies and Farm Productivity in Thailand.* Baltimore, Md.: Johns Hopkins University Press.

Feeny, David. 1988. "Agricultural Expansion and Forest Depletion in Thailand, 1900–1975." In John F. Richards and Richard P. Tucker. *World Deforestation in the Twentieth Century.* Durham, N.C.: Duke University Press.

Feeny, David, Filkret Berkes, Bonnie J. McCay, and James M. Acheson. 1990. "The Tragedy of the Commons: Twenty-Two Years Later." *Human Ecology* 18(1): 1–19.

Field, B.C. 1989. "The Evolution of Property Rights." *Kyklos* 42: 319–45.

Ford Foundation. 1989. *Alternativas ao Desmatamento na Amazônia: Conservação dos Recursos Naturais.* 2d edition. New York.

Foweraker, Joe. 1981. *The Struggle for Land: A Political Economy of the Pioneer Frontier in Brazil from 1930 to the Present Day.* New York: Cambridge University Press.

França Ribeiro, Ueliton, and Paulo Rodolfo Leopoldo. 1989. "Colonização ao Longo da Transamazônica: Trecho Km 930-1035." *Interciencia* 14(6): 311–16.

Furze, Brian. 1992. "Ecologically Sustainable Rural Development and the Difficulty of Social Change." *Environmental Values* 1: 141–55.

Garcia, Afranio Raul Jr. 1990. *O Sul: Caminho do Roçado. Estratégias de Reprodução Camponesa e Tranformação Social.* Brasília: Editora Universidade de Brasília.

Geertz, Clifford. 1963. *Agricultural Involution: The Process of Ecological Change in Indonesia.* Berkeley, Calif.: University of California Press.

Gillis, Malcolm, and Robert Repetto, eds. 1988. *Public Policies and the Misuse of Forest Resources.* New York: Cambridge University Press.

Goodland, Robert. 1991. "Tropical Deforestation Solutions, Ethics and Religions." Environment Department Working Paper 43. World Bank, Washington, D.C.

———. 1992. "Environmental Priorities for Financing Institutions." *Environmental Conservation* 19(1).

Goodland, Robert, and Herman Daly. 1993. "Poverty Alleviation is Essential for Environmental Sustainability." Working Paper 1993–42. Environment Department, World Bank, Washington, D.C.

Goodland, Robert, Herman Daly, and Salah El Serafy. 1992. "The Urgent Need for a Rapid Transition to Global Environmental Sustainability." Environment Department, World Bank, Washington, D.C.

Goodman, David, and Anthony Hall, eds. 1990. *The Future of Amazonia: Destruction or Sustainable Development?* New York: St. Martin's Press.

Gradwohl, Judith, and Russel Greenberg. 1988. *Saving the Tropical Forests.* Washington, D.C.: Island Press.

Gregersen, Hans, Peter Oram, and others, eds. *Priorities for Forestry and Agroforestry Policy Research: Report of an International Workshop.* Washington, D.C.: International Food Policy Research Institute.

Gross, Anthony. 1990. "Amazonia in the Nineties: Sustainable Development or Another Decade of Destruction?" *Third World Quarterly* 12: 3-4.

Guzmán, Rolando M., and Eustáquio J. Reis. 1992. "An Econometric Model of the Amazon Deforestation." Discussion Paper 265. Instidue de Pesquisa Economica Aplicada, Rio de Janeiro.

Hall, Anthony. 1989. *Developing Amazonia: Deforestation and Social Conflict in Brazil's Carajas Programme.* New York: Manchester University Press.

Hansen, Stein. 1988. "Debt for Nature Swaps: Overview and Discussion of Key Issues." Environment Department Working Paper 1. World Bank, Washington, D.C.

Harley, J. L., and F. Le Tacon. 1990. " Deforestation in the Tropics and Proposals to Arrest It." *AMBIO* 19(8): 372–78.

Hébette, Jean, ed. 1991. *O Cerco Está se Fechando.* Petrópolis/Rio de Janeiro: Editora Vozes.

Hébette, Jean, and Rosa E.A. Marin. 1977. *Colonização espontanea, politica agraria e grupos sociais.* Belem, Pará: University of Pará.

Hecht, Susanna. 1981. "Deforestation in the Amazon Basin: Magnitude, Dynamics and Social Resource Effects." *Studies in Third World Societies* 13: 61.

Hecht, Susanna B., Richard Nirgaard, and others. 1988. "The Economics of Cattle Ranching in Eastern Amazonia." *Interciencia* 13(5): 233–40.

Helmsing, Bert. 1982. "Agricultural Production in the Periphery: Settlements Schemes Reconsidered." *Development and Change* 13(1): 401.

———. 1983. "Colonos, Agricultural Colonization and Production in Andean Countries." Working Paper Series 10, Institute of Social Studies.

Hemming, John, ed. 1985a. *Change in the Amazon Basin, Volume I: Man's Impact on Forests and Rivers.* New York: Manchester University Press.

———. 1985b. *Change in the Amazon Basin, Volume II: The Frontier After a Decade of Colonization.* Symposium held at the 44th International Congress of Americanists, Manchester, U.K., September 1982. New York: Manchester University Press.

Hernandez, Alejandro. 1984. "Migración de Colonos en Darién." In Alberto McKay and Stanley Heckadon Moreño, eds., *Colonización y Destrucción de Bosques en Panamá*. Panama: Asociacíon Panameña de Antropologia.

Horowitz, Michael, and Peter D. Little, eds. 1987. *Lands at Risk in the Third World: Local-Level Perspectives*. Boulder, Colo.: Westview Press.

Hsiao, Cheng. 1986. *Analysis of Panel Data*. Econometric Society Monographs. Cambridge, U.K.: Cambridge University Press.

Ianni, Octavio. 1979. "Colonizacao e Contra-Reforma Agraria na Amazônia." *Colecao Sociologia Brasileira* 11. Petropolis, Brazil: Editora Vozes.

Inter-American Development Bank. 1970. "Evaluation of Tropical Colonization Projects in Latin America." Papers on Agricultural Development No. 7. Washington, D.C.

Janz, Klaus, Jean-Paul Lanly, and Deo Singh. 1991. "FAO's 1990 Reassessment of Tropical Forest Cover." *Nature and Resources* 27(2): 21–26.

Jessup, Timothy C., and Nancy Lee Peluso. 1986. "Minor Forest Products as Common Property Resources in East Kalimantan, Indonesia." *Proceedings of the Conference on Common Property Resource Management*. Washington, D.C.: National Academy Press.

Jones, Donald, Virginia Dale, John Beauchamp, Marcos Pedlowski, and Rober O'Neill. 1992. "Farming in Rondônia." U.S Department of Energy, Washington, D.C.

Jones, Jeffrey. 1990. *Colonization and Environment: Land Settlement Projects in Central America*. Tokyo: United Nations University Press.

Junk, Wolfgang J. 1989. "The Use of Amazonian Floodplains under an Ecological Perspective." *Interciencia* 14(6): 317–22.

Katzman, Martin. 1977. *Cities and Frontiers in Brazil: Regional Dimensions of Economic Development*. Cambridge, Mass.: Harvard University Press.

Kelly, Brian, and Mark London. 1983. *Amazon*. New York: Holt, Rinehart, and Winston.

Kneerim, Jill. 1980. *Village Women Organize: The Mraru Bus Service*. New York: SEEDS.

Kolhepp, Gerd, and Achim Schrader, eds. 1987. *Homen e Natureza na Amazônia*. Simpósio Internacional e Interdisciplinar, Blaubeuren, 1986. Tubinger Geographisches Studien, Blaubeuren.

Lal, R. 1989. "Potential of Agroforestry as a Sustainable Alternative to Shifting Cultivation: Concluding Remarks." *Agroforestry Systems* 8: 239–42.

Lamb, David. 1991. "Combining Traditional and Commercial Uses of Rain Forests." *Nature and Resources* 27(2): 3–11.

Lavinas, Lena, ed. 1987. *A Urbanização da Fronteira*. Volumes 1 and 2. Rio de Janeiro: Publipur.

Levi, Yair. 1984. "Settlers' Organizations and the Settlement Community: Relationships Emerging in New Land Settlement Projects." *Journal of Rural Cooperation* 12(1–2): 25.

Lin, Justin Yifu, and Jeffrey Nugent. 1994. "Institutions and Economic Development." In Jere Behrman and T. N. Srinivasan, eds., *Handbook of Development Economics*. Amsterdam: North Holland.

Lisansky, Elizabeth. 1990. *Migrants to Amazonia: Spontaneous Colonization in the Brazilian Frontier*. Boulder, Colo.: Westview Press.

Livernash, Robert. 1992. "The Growing Influence of NGOs in the Developing World." *Environment* 34(5): 13–43.

Lopez, Ramon. 1992. "Environmental Degradation and Economic Openness in LDCs: The Poverty Linkage." *American Journal of Agricultural Economics* December: 1138–1143.

Lopez, Ramon, and Mario Niklitschek. 1991. "Dual Economic Growth in Poor Tropical Areas." *Journal of Development Economics* 36: 189–211.

Loureiro, Violeta. 1985. *Os Parceiros do Mar: Natureza e Conflito Social na Pesca da Amazônia, Belém, Pará*. Brazil: Coselho Nacional de Desenvolvimento Científico e Tecnológico.

———. 1987. *Miséria da Ascensão Social: Capitalismo e Pequena Produção na Amazônia*. São Paulo: Editora Marco Zero.

Lovejoy, Thomas, and Ghillean Prance, eds. 1985. *Amazonia: Key Environments*. New York: Pergamon Press.

Luoma, Jon. 1992. "New Government Plan for National Forests Generates a Debate." *The New York Times*, June 30, page C4.

Lutz, Ernst, and Mohan Munasinghe. 1991. "Environmental-Economic Evaluation of Projects and Policies for Sustainable Development." Environment Department Working Paper 42. World Bank, Washington, D.C.

Maddala, G. F. 1983. *Limited-Dependent and Qualitative Variables in Econometrics*. Econometrics Society Monographs. Cambridge, U.K.: Cambridge University Press.

Magrath, William. 1989. "The Challenge of the Commons: The Allocation of Nonexclusive Resources." Environment Department Working Paper 14. World Bank, Washington, D.C.

Mahar, Dennis. 1979. *Frontier Development Policy in Brazil: A Study of Amazonia*. New York: Praeger Publishers.

———. 1981. *Brazil: Integrated Development of the Northwest Frontier*. World Bank Country Study. Washington, D.C.

———. 1989. *Government Policies and Deforestation in Brazil's Amazon Region*. Washington, D.C.: World Bank.

Mahony, Rhona. 1992. "Debt-For-Nature-Swaps, Who Really Benefits?" *The Ecologist* 22(3): 99-103.

Manshard, Walther, and Willian B. Morgan, eds. 1988. *Agricultural Expansion and Pioneer Settlements in Humid Tropics*. Tokyo: United Nations University Press.

Margolis, Maxine. 1973. *The Moving Frontier: Social Economic Change in a Southern Brazilian Community*. Gainesville, : University of Florida Press.

Markandya, Anil, and David Pearce. 1988. "Environmental Considerations and the Choice Discount Rate in Developing Countries." Environment Discussion Paper 3. World Bank, Washington, D.C.

Marques, Fabricio. 1993. "Limite Imaginario." *Veja* 26(22).

Martine, George, ed. 1985. *Biotecnologia e Sociedade: O Caso Brasileiro*. São Paulo: Editora da UNICAMP.

———. 1992a. "Processos Recentes de Concentração e Desconcentração Urbana no Brazil: Determinantes e Implicacoes." Brasilia: Instituto SPN.

————. 1992b. "The Recent Trends Toward Deconcentration and Demetropolization in Brazil." Paper prepared for the 1993 IUSSP General Conference, Montreal, Canada.

————. 1992c. "Fases e Faces da Modernização Agrícola Brasileira." *Planejamento e Politicas Públicas* 3: 3-44.

Martine, George, and Liscio Camargo. 1983. *Crescimento e Distribuição da População Brasileira: Tendencias Recentes.* Discussion Paper 5/82. Brasilia: IPEA/PNUD.

Martine, George, and Vilmar Faria. 1988. "Impacts of Social Research on Policy Formulation: Lessons from the Brazilian Experience in the Population Field." *The Journal of Developing Areas* 23: 43–62.

Mattos, M. M., C. Uhl, and D. A. Goncalves. 1992. *Economic and Ecological Perspectives on Ranching in the Eastern Amazon in the 1990s.* Belem, Brazil: Imazon.

McMillan, Della, Thomas Painter, and others. 1990. "Settlement Experiences and Development Strategies in the Onchocerciasis Controlled Areas of West Africa—Final Report." *Land Settlement Review.* New York: Institute for Development Anthropology.

Mesquita, Olindina Vianna, and Solange Tietzman Silva. 1987a. "A Evolução da Agricultura Brasileira na Decada de 70." *Revista Brasileira de Geografia* 1(49): 3–10.

————. 1987b. "A Evolução da Agricultura Brasileira na Regiao Sul na Decada de 70." *Revista Brasileira de Geografia* 1(49): 159–95.

————. 1987c. "Da Policultura Regional a Hegemonia da Soja—O Oeste do Paraná em Questao." *Revista Brasileira de Geografia* 105 (January/June): 155–70.

Millikan, Brent. 1992. "Tropical Deforestation, Land Degradation, and Society: Lessons from Rondônia." *Latin American Perspectives* 19(1): 45–72.

Mink, Stephen D. 1993. *Poverty, Population, and the Environment.* Discussion Paper 189. Washington, D.C.: World Bank.

Monteiro de Barros, Henrique O. 1991. "Small Commodity Agriculture in Northeast Brazil: The Case of Horticultural Farming in Pernambuco Brejos." Ph.D. dissertation, University of London.

Moran, Emilio. 1975. "Pioneer Farmers of the Transamazon Highway: Adaptation and Agricultural Production in the Lowland Tropics." Ph.D. Dissertation, University of Florida, Gainesville, Fl.

————. 1982. "Ecological, Anthropological and Agronomic Research in the Amazon Basin." *Latin American Research Review* 17(1): 3–41.

————. 1983. *The Dilemma of Amazonian Development.* Boulder, Colo.: Westview Press.

————, ed. 1989. *The Dilemma of Amazonian Development.* Boulder, Colo.: Westview Press.

Mueller, Charles C. 1992. "Centro-Oeste: Evolução, Situação Atual e Perspectivas de Desenvolvimento Sustentavel." *A Ecologia e o Novo Padrao de Desenvolvimento no Brasil* 89–129.

Munasinghe, Mohan. 1992. "Environmental Economics and Valuation in Development Decisionmaking." Environment Department Working Paper 51. World Bank, Washington, D.C.

Murgueitio, Enrique. 1990. "Intensive Sustainable Livestock Production: An Alternative to Tropical Deforestation." *AMBIO* 19(8): 397–400.

Musumecci, L. 1988. *O mito da terra liberta; colonização espontânea, campesinato, e patronágem na Amazônia Oriental.* São Paulo: ANPOCS/Vértice.

Myers, Norman. 1988. "Natural Resource System and Human Exploitation Systems: Physiobiotic and Ecological Linkages." Environment Department Working Paper 12. World Bank, Washington, D.C.

Nelson, Michael. 1973. *The Development of Tropical Lands: Policy Issues in Latin America.* Baltimore, Md.: Johns Hopkins University Press.

Nicholaides, J.J., and others. 1985. "Agricultural Alternatives for the Amazon Basin." *Bioscience* 35(1): 279–85.

North, Douglass. 1990. *Institutions, Institutional Change, and Economic Performance.* New York: Cambridge University Press.

Oberai, A. S., ed. 1988. *Land Settlement Policies and Population Redistribution in Developing Countries: Achievements, Problems, and Prospects.* New York: Praeger Publishers.

Oliveira, Francisco de. 1981. *Elegia para uma Religiao.* Rio de Janeiro: Ed. Paz e Terra.

Ozório de Almeida, Anna Luíza, ed. 1984. *Biotecnologia e Agricultura: Perspectivas para o Caso Brasileiro.* Rio de Janeiro: Editora Vozes.

———. 1985. "Atribulações de uma Economista na Amazônia." *Ciência Hoje* 3(16): 67–74.

———. 1987. "Os Comerciantes da Fronteira." Texto para discussão 149. Instituto de Economia Industrial. Rio de Janeiro: UFRJ.

———. 1989. "Colonizing the Amazon." *Hemisphere* 1(3): 24–25.

———. 1990a. *A Colonização Oficial na Amazônia nos Anos 80.* Texto para Discussão 207. Rio de Janeiro-Brasilia: IPEA.

———. 1990b. *A Colonização Particular na Amazônia nos Anos 80.* Texto para Discussão 208. Rio de Janeiro-Brasilia: IPEA.

———. 1990c. "A Biotecnologia no Brasil: Desenvolvimentos Recentes." *Ciência e Tecnologia* 83(5): 545–70.

———, ed. 1990d. "Biotecnologia: Situação e Perspectives. Resultados Preliminares." *Cadernos de Economia 2.* Rio de Janeiro/Brasília: IPEA.

———. 1991a. "Colonização na Amazônia: Reforma Agrária numa Fronteira Internacional." *Perspectivas da Economia Brasileira -1992.* Rio de Janeiro-Brasilia: IPEA.

———. 1991b. "Debt Peonage and Over-Deforestation in the Brazilian Amazon." From the proceedings of the meeting of the International Agricultural Economics Association, August. Tokyo.

———. 1992. *The Colonization of the Amazon.* Austin: University of Texas at Austin Press.

Ozório de Almeida, Anna Luíza, and Carlos Eduardo Rebello de Mendonça. 1989. "A Pequena Produção: Uma Visão Unificada." *Estudos Econômicos* 19: 9–23.

Ozório de Almeida, Anna Luíza, Angela Moulin Penalva Santos, Adriana F. Alves, and Maria da Piedade Morais. 1992. *A Colonização Sustentável na Amazônia.* Texto para Discussão 266. Rio de Janeiro-Brasilia: IPEA.

Ozório de Almeida, Anna Luíza, and Charley F. Velloso dos Santos. 1990a. "A Colonização Oficial na Amazônia nos Anos 80." Texto para Discussão 207. Rio de Janeiro/Brasília: IPEA.

———. 1990b. "A Colonização Particular na Amazônia nos Anos 80." Textos para Discussao 208. Rio de Janeiro/Brasília: IPEA.

Ozório de Almeida, Anna Luíza, and S. Graham. 1994. "Regulatory Costs and Employment in the Informal Sector in Argentina." Education and Social Policy Discussion Paper 45. World Bank, Washington, D.C.

Padoch, C. 1980. "The Environmental and Demographic Effects of Alternative Cash-Producing Activities Among Shifting Cultivators in Sarawak." Tropical Ecology and Development, Department of Botany, Banaras Hindu University, Vanarasi, India.

Padoch, C., and Andrew P. Vayda. 1983. "Patterns of Resource Use and Human Settlement in Tropical Forests." In F. B. Golley, ed., *Tropical Rain Forest Ecosystems: Structure and Function*. Lausanne: Elsevier Scientific Publishing Company.

Padoch, C., J. Chota, and others. 1985. "Amazonian Agroforestry: A Market-Oriented System in Peru." *Agroforestry Systems* 3: 47–58.

Palm, Ola, and Klas Sandell. 1989. "Sustainable Agriculture and Nitrogen Supply in Sri Lanka: Farmers' and Scientists' Perspective." *AMBIO* 18(8): 442–48.

Paris, R., and I. Ruzicka. 1991. "Barking Up the Wrong Tree: The Role of Rent Appropriation in Sustainable Tropical Forest Management." Asian Development Bank, Environment Office Occasional Paper 1. Manila.

Partridge, William, and Debra Schumman. 1989. *The Human Ecology of Tropical Land Settlement in Latin America*. Boulder, Colo.: Westview Press.

Pearce, David, and Giles Atkinson. 1993. "Measuring Sustainable Development." *Ecodecision* 9 (June).

Pearce, David, and Anil Markandya. 1989. "Marginal Opportunity Cost as a Planning Concept in Natural Resources Management." In Gunter Schramm and Jeremy Warford, eds., *Environmental Management and Economic Development*. Baltimore, Md.: Johns Hopkins University Press.

Pearce, David, and Douglas Southgate. 1988. "Agricultural Colonization and Environmental Degradation in Frontier Developing Economies." Environment Department Working Paper 9. World Bank, Washington, D.C.

Pearce, David, and Jeremy J. Warford. 1993. *World Without End: Economics, Environment, and Sustainable Development*. New York: Oxford University Press.

Penalva Santos, Angela Moulin S. 1993. "Comércio Fronteira de Negocios na Colonizacao da Amazonia." Rio de Janeiro: IPEA/PNUD-BRA.

Peuker, Axel. 1992. "Public Policies and Deforestation: A Case Study of Costa Rica." Report 14. Latin America and the Caribbean Technical Department, World Bank, Washington, D.C.

Pezzey, John. 1989. "Economic Analysis of Sustainable Growth and Sustainable Development." Environment Department Working Paper 15. World Bank, Washington, D.C.

———. 1992. *Sustainable Development Concepts: An Economic Analysis*. World Bank Environment Paper No. 2. Washington, D.C.

Poelhekke, Fábio G. M. N. 1986. "Fences in the Jungle: Cattle Raising and the Economic and Social Integration of the Amazon Region in Brazil." *Revista Geográfica* (Instituto Pan-Americano de Geografia e História) 104: 33–43.

Porto Tavares, Vania, and others. 1972. *Colonização Dirigida no Brasil: Suas Possibilidades na Regiao Amazonica*. Rio de Janeiro: IPEA.

Prosterman, R.L., ed. 1990. *Agrarian Reform and Grassroots Development: Ten Case Studies*. Seattle: University of Washington.

Redclift, Michael. 1986. "Sustainability and the Market: Survival Strategies on the Bolivian Frontier." *The Journal of Development Studies* 23(1): 93–105.

———. 1987. *Sustainable Development: Exploring the Contradictions.* New York: Methuen.

dos Reis Velloso, João Paulo, ed. 1992. *A Ecologia e o Novo Padrão de Desenvolvimento no Brasil.* São Paulo: Nobel.

Renkow, Mitch. 1993. "Land Prices, Land Rents, and Technological Change: Evidence from Pakistan." *World Development* 21(5).

Rensberger, Boyce. 1993. "Environment: Tropical Deforestation's Other Side." *The Washington Post.* September 20.

Repetto, Robert. 1989. "Economic Incentives for Sustainable Production." In Gunter Schramm and Jeremy Warford, eds., *Environmental Management and Economic Development.* Baltimore. Md.: Johns Hopkins University Press.

Rezende, Gervasio Castro de. 1981. "Credito Rural Subsidiado e Preco da Terra no Brasil." Texto para Discussao Interna 41. Rio de Janeiro: IPEA/INPES.

Romanoff, Steven. 1992. "Food and Debt Among Rubber Tappers in the Bolivian Amazon." *Human Organization* 51(2): 122–35.

Sadan, E. 1985. "Settlement, Rehabilitation and Reform: Dilemmas in Agricultural Development Projects in Latin America." *Journal of Rural Cooperation* 13(2): 135–48.

Sanchez, Pedro A. 1991. "Alternatives to Slash and Burn: A Pragmatic Approach to Mitigate Tropical Deforestation." Paper presented at a World Bank conference on "Agricultural Technology for Sustainable Economic Development in the New Century: Policy Issues for the International Community." Airlie House, Virginia. October 23.

Serageldin, Ismail. 1993. *Development Partners: Aid and Cooperation in the 1990s.* Washington, D.C.: SIDA.

Sawyer, Donald. 1990. "Migration and Urban Development in the Amazon." Paper prepared for the World Bank as part of a critical literature review on Amazonian migrations. World Bank, Washington, D.C.

Schmidt, R. 1987. "Tropical Rain Forest Management." UNASYVA 39(2): 2–17.

Schmink, Marianne, and Charles Wood. 1979. "Blaming the Victim: Small Farmer Production in an Amazonian Colonization Project." *Studies in Third World Societies* 7(77).

———, eds. 1984. *Frontier Expansion in Amazonia.* Gainesville: The University of Florida Press.

———. 1992. *Contested Frontiers in Amazonia.* New York: Columbia University Press.

Schneider, Robert R. 1991. "An Analysis of Environmental Problems and Policies in the Amazon." Paper presented at the Seminário sobre Politicas y Practicas para Desarrollo Sostenible en los Paises Miembros del Tratado de Cooperacion Amazonica. Caracas, Venezuela, October 21–25.

———. 1993. "Land Abandonment, Property Rights, and Agricultural Sustainability in the Amazon." Latin America and the Caribbean Department, Dissemination Note No. III. World Bank, Washington, D.C.

Schonkwiler, J. Scott, and Timothy G. Taylor. 1986. "Alternative Stochastic Specifications of the Frontier Production Function in the Analysis of Agricultural Credit Programs and Technical Efficiency." *Journal of Development Economics* 21: 149–60.

Serôa da Motta, Ronaldo. 1991. "Recent Evolution of Environmental Management in the Brazilian Public Sector: Issues and Recommendations." In D. Erocal, ed., *Environmental Management in Developing Countries*. Paris: OECD.

———. 1992a. "Perdas e Serviços Ambientais do Recurso Água para Uso Doméstico." IPEA, Rio de Janeiro.

———. 1992b. "Some Comments on Depletion and Degradation Costs on Income Measurement." IPEA, Rio de Janeiro.

Serôa da Motta, Ronaldo, and Peter Herman May. 1992. "Loss in Forest Resource Values due to Agricultural Land Conversion in Brazil." IPEA, Rio de Janeiro.

Serôa da Motta, Ronaldo, and Eustaquio Reis. 1994. "The Application of Economic Instruments in Environmetal Policy: The Brazilian Case." OECD/UNEP workshop paper. Paris. May 26–27.

Serôa da Motta, Ronaldo, and Carlos Eduardo Frickman Young. 1991. "Natural Resources and National Accounts: Sustainable Income from Mineral Extraction in Brazil." Rio de Janeiro: IPEA

Serra, José, and José Roberto R. Afonso. 1993. "Financas Publicas Municipais II: Trajetoria e Mitos." *Conjuntura Economica*. November/December: 35–43.

Shah, Anwar. 1990. "The New Fiscal Federalism in Brazil." Working Paper 557. World Bank, Washington, D.C.

Sikking, Kathryn. 1991. *Ideas and Institutions: Developmentalism in Brazil and Argentina*. Ithaca, N.Y: Cornell University Press.

Sioli, Harold. 1989. "Introdução ao Simpósio 'Amazônia: Deflorestamento e Possíveis Efeitos'." *Interciencia* 14(6): 286–0.

Smith, Nigel J. H. 1982. *Rainforest Corridors: The Transamazon Colonization Scheme*. Berkeley: University of California Press.

Socolik, Helio. 1989. "O Fundo de Participacao dos Municipios." *Conjuntura Economica* December: 51-58.

Southgate, Douglas. 1990. "The Causes of Land Degradation along 'Spontaneously' Expanding Agricultural Frontiers in the Third World." *Land Economics* 66(1): 93–101.

———. 1991. "Tropical Deforestation and Agricultural Development in Latin America." Environment Department Working Paper 1991-20. World Bank, Washington, D.C.

———. 1992. "Policies Contributing to Agricultural Colonization of Latin America's Tropical Forests." In Narendra Sharma, ed., *Managing the World's Forests: Looking for Balance Between Conservation and Development*. Dubuque, Iowa: Kendall/Hunt Publishing Company.

Southgate, Douglas, and David Pearce. 1988. "Agricultural Colonization and Environmental Degradation in Frontier Developing Economies." Environment Department Working Paper 9. World Bank, Washington, D.C.

Spears, John. 1988. "Containing Tropical Deforestation: A Review of Priority Areas for Technological and Policy Research." Environment Department Working Paper 10, World Bank, Washington, D.C.

Speth, James Gustave. 1992. "On the Road to Rio and to Sustainability." *Environmental Science and Technology* 26(6): 1075–76.

Stirling, Andrew. 1993. "Environmental Valuation: How Much is the Emperor Wearing?" *The Ecologist* 23(3).

Strong, Maurice F. 1992. "The Promises and Challenges of UNCED '92." *Ocean and Coastal Management* 18: 5–14.

Sung, Woonki, and Rosaria Troia. 1992. *Developments in Debt Conversion Programs and Conversion Activities.* World Bank Technical Paper 170. Washington, D.C.

Thapa, Gopal. 1990. "Actors and Factors of Deforestation in 'Tropical Asia'." *Environmental Conservation* 17(1): 19–27.

Thapa, Gopal, and Karl E. Weber. 1989. "Land Settlement in Tropical Asia." *Habitat International* 13(4): 147–60.

Thiele, Graham. 1990. *Are Peasant Farming Systems in the Amazon Sustainable?* Discussion Paper 282. Brighton, England: Institute of Development Studies.

Thomson, James T., David Feeny, and Ronald Oakerson. 1992. "Institutional Dynamics: The Evolution and Dissolution of Common Property Resource Management." In Bromley, Daniel, David Feeny, and others, eds. *Making the Commons Work.* San Francisco, Calif.: ICS Press.

Tisdell, Clem. 1988. "Sustainable Development: Different Perspectives of Ecologists and Economists, and Relevance to LDCs." *World Development* 16(3): 373–84.

Tulchin, Joseph S., ed. 1991. *Economic Development & Environmental Protection in Latin America.* Boulder, Colo.: Lynne Rienner Publishers.

Uhl, C., A. Verissimo, P. Barreto, and R. Tarifa. 1992. "A Evolução da Fronteira Amazonica: Oportunidades para um Desenvolvimento Sustentavel." *Para Desenvolvimento* June: 13–31.

Uhl, C., A. Verissimo, M. M. Mattos, Z. Brandino, and I. C. G. Vieira. 1991. "Social, Economic, and Ecological Consequences of Selective Logging in an Amazon Frontier: The Case of Tailandia." *Forest Ecology and Management* 46: 243–73.

Van Vliet, Klaas Geert. 1989. "Eco and Ethnodevelopment, Geopolitics and Situational Planning: Perspectives for Alternative Discourse and Praxis in the Amazon Basin." *Interciencia* 14(6): 304–10.

Velho, O. 1981. *Frentes de Expansão e Estrutura Agrária: Estudo do Processo de Penetração numa Area da Transamazica.* Rio de Janeiro: Zahar.

Verissimo, A., P. Barreto, M. M. Mattos, and R. Tarifa. 1992. *Impactos da Atividade Madereira e Perspectivas para o Manejo Sustentavel da Floresta numa Velha Fronteira da Amazonia: o Caso de Paragominas.* Belem, Brazil: Imazon.

Villalobos, Arturo. 1982. "Small Farmers' Production Systems and the Improvement of Agriculture in Central America." *Agricultural System* 8:209–17.

Vosti, Stephen A. 1992. "Constraints to Improved Food Security: Linkages Among Agriculture, Environment, and Poverty." Paper prepared for the IFPRI Food Policy Workshop on Famine and Drought Mitigation in Ethiopia in the 1990s. Addis Ababa, Ethiopia, July 2–3. Ministry of Economic Planning.

Vosti, Stephen A., Thomas Reardon, and others. 1991. *Agricultural Sustainability, Growth, and Poverty Alleviation: Issues and Policies.* Washington, D.C.: Food and Agriculture Development Centre.

Wachter, Daniel. 1992. "Land Tilling for Land Conservation in Developing Countries?" Working Paper 1992-8. World Bank, Washington, D.C.

Weil, Connie, and Jim Weil. 1983. "Government, Campesinos, and Business in the Bolivian Chapare: A Case Study of Amazonian Occupation." *Inter-American Economic Affairs* 36(4): 29–62.

Wells, Michael. 1991. "Trust Funds and Endowments as a Biodiversity Conservation Tool." Environment Department Working Paper 1991-26. World Bank, Washington, D.C.

Wesche, Rolf, and Thomas Bruneau. 1990. *Integration and Change in Brazil's Middle Amazon*. Ottawa: University of Ottawa Press.

Wirth, John, and others. 1987. *State and Society in Brazil: Continuity and Change*. Boulder, Colo.: Westiew Press.

Wood, William B. 1990. "Tropical Deforestation." *Global Environmental Change* 1(1): 23–41.

World Bank. 1978. *Agricultural Land Settlement*. A World Bank Issues Paper. Washington, D.C.

———. 1989. *Renewable Resource Management in Agriculture*. A World Bank Operations Evaluation Study. Washington, D.C.

———. 1990. *Evaluation Results for 1988*. A World Bank Operations Evaluation Study. Washington, D.C.

———. 1991a. *Environmental Assessment Sourcebook. Volume 1: Policies, Procedures, and Cross-Sectoral Issues*. Technical Paper 139. Washington, D.C.

———. 1991b. *Environmental Assessment Sourcebook. Volume 3: Guidelines for Environmental Assessment of Energy and Industry Projects*. Technical Paper 154. Washington, D.C.

———. 1991c. "Forest Policy Paper." Agricultural and Rural Development Department, World Bank, Washington, D.C.

———. 1991d *The Forest Sector*. A World Bank Policy Paper. Washington, D.C.

———. 1991e. *The World Bank and the Environment: A Progress Report, Fiscal 1991*. Washington, D.C.

———. 1992a. "Environment and Development in Latin America and the Caribbean—The Role of the World Bank." Latin American and Caribbean Department, World Bank, Washington, D.C.

———. 1992b. *Population and the World Bank: Implications From Eight Case Studies*. Washington, D.C.: World Bank.

———. 1992c. *World Development Report 1992: Development and the Environment*. New York: Oxford University Press.

———. 1992d. *World Bank and the Environment 1992*. Washington, D.C.

———. 1993a. "Early Experience with Involuntary Resettlement: Overview." World Bank, Operations Evaluation Department, Washington, D.C.

———. 1993b. "Pilot Program to Conserve the Brazilian Rain Forest, Background Materials for the Press."

———. 1993c. "Rain Forest Pilot Program Update."

———. 1994a. "Indonesia Transmigration Program: A Review of Five Bank-Supported Projects." Operations and Evaluation Department.

———. 1994b. *Making Development Sustainable: The World Bank Group and the Environment, Fiscal 1994*.

———. 1995. *Mainstreaming the Environment: The World Bank Group and the Environment since the Rio Earth Summit, Fiscal 1995*.

Young, Carlos E. F. 1994. "Mr. Keynes and the Environment: An Application of the Use-Cost Concept to the Deforestation Problem." University College of London.

Zweede, Johan. 1993. "Sustained Yield Forest Management (SYFM) in the Eastern Amazon." Seminar paper, World Bank, August 17.

Index